deep north

stories of somali resettlement in vermont

Shadir Mohamed, Fardusa A. Abdo,
& Abdihamid A. Muhumed

collected, edited, & afterword by
Brad Kessler

photographs by Dona Ann McAdams

Onion River Press

Onion River Press

24 Maple Street, Suite 214

Burlington, VT 05401

www.onionriverpress.com

ISBN: 978-1-9571-8438-8

Publisher's Cataloging-in-Publication data

Names: Mohamed, Shadir, author. | Abdo, Fardusa A., author. | Muhumed, Abdihamid A., author. | Kessler, Brad, editor. | McAdams, Dona Ann, photographer.
Title: Deep north : stories of Somali resettlement in Vermont / Shadir Mohamed; Fardusa A. Abdo; & Abdihamid A . Muhumed ; collected, edited, & afterword by Brad Kessler; photographs by Dona Ann McAdams.
Description: Burlington, VT: Onion River Press, 2023.
Identifiers: LCCN: 2023914143 | ISBN: 978-1-957184-38-8
Subjects: LCSH Refugees--Somalia--Biography. | Refugees--Vermont--Biography. | Refugees--United States--Biography. | BISAC BIOGRAPHY & AUTOBIOGRAPHY / Personal Memoirs | BIOGRAPHY & AUTOBIOGRAPHY / Cultural, Ethnic & Regional / African American & Black | HISTORY / Africa / East
Classification: LCC HV640.5.S8 .M64 2023 | DDC 362.87096773/092--dc23

The Jubba River feeds the farmland of the Somali Bantu.

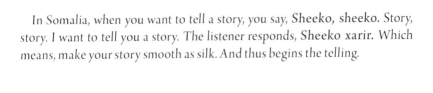

In Somalia, when you want to tell a story, you say, Sheeko, sheeko. Story, story. I want to tell you a story. The listener responds, Sheeko xarir. Which means, make your story smooth as silk. And thus begins the telling.

Contents

Shadir

We had traveled a long way, through many countries and time zones. It was the first time on a plane for me and my wife Amina and our four children Safia, Haji, Fardumo, and our youngest then, Gemana, who was just eight weeks old. We brought with us nearly nothing. Only a few items of clothes from the camp in Kenya, not even my Koran. Between the six of us we had one bag. When the plane took off in Nairobi, Fardumo cried. She wanted to go "back home." How could I tell her we had no home yet? She knew nothing of our real home in Somalia. She'd lived only in refugee camps. But we were heading now to a place we hoped to be home.

There were forty other refugee families on our flight, a big Delta airplane, all of us Somali Bantu. We changed planes in Brussels then flew across the ocean and arrived at JFK in New York late in the afternoon. Some of the families were going on to other cities: Boston or Atlanta. Minneapolis. St. Louis. We were the only family in the whole group heading to Vermont. No one had ever heard of the place before. No one knew exactly where it was.

At JFK, an American man who'd been helping us found the bus to LaGuardia. The children were amazed at New York. They'd never seen so many white people before. At LaGuardia we waited until night and took a smaller plane north. The flight was short. There were hardly any lights below in Burlington. It was winter. December 15, 2004. A day I'll remember forever.

In Vermont it was dark and like 20 degrees outside. We'd never felt such cold before, even inside the airport we were cold and very tired. Our host family Linda and Chris Miller were waiting for us with Judy and Raga from the Vermont Refugee and Resettlement Program. They knew our names and the names of all our children. Judy welcomed us so warmly, as if she'd known us for years. I couldn't figure out how she knew all of us by sight. I found out later: She'd had our photographs beforehand and memorized our names!

Linda and Chris brought us winter coats. They knew we'd be cold. They took us out to the cars and we drove to their house in North Hero. Judy and Raga came in another car. They showed us inside the house: the bathroom sink, the hot and cold water, and how to use a toilet, because we'd never seen these things before. We ate some American food, which was a little hard for us, everything so strange-tasting and new. But the Millers gave us a room big enough for the whole family and we felt safe. By the time Judy and Raga left, it was early in the morning and we all finally fell to sleep.

We moved into our first American home a few weeks later. 40 Intervale Avenue in Burlington, Vermont. There were two bedrooms, a kitchen, a bathroom. Because we were a family of six, people said we needed a larger apartment. But I said our apartment was big enough. In all the places we'd lived since fleeing Somalia, we'd never had a home so large with so much room. We'd lived so long in the camps, sometimes only with a piece of plastic over our heads. So the apartment at 40 Intervale seemed luxurious. It cost eight hundred dollars a month to rent. I didn't really understand the concept of rent at first. We had just arrived and I had no job and I had to pay $800 for a place to sleep. The resettlement program gave us $903 each month. That seemed like a large amount of money! But the rent for the apartment was $800 and then we had to pay heat, which was $400 each month, and electricity, which was around $20. All of that added up $1,223 dollars a month. And that was before paying for any food. How would we survive in Vermont?

When I couldn't pay the gas, the company disconnected the gas. It was winter. We had no heat. We couldn't cook. Rashid Hussein at the Vermont Resettlement Program told me about a place called Community Action and they helped cover part of the bills. Now, after paying rent and the reduced prices for heat, we had $103 left over for food for six people for a month. How could that work? We paid for the food to eat, and not the gas. So they cut the gas off again and we had no heat. In the meantime, I kept looking for a job. Then the resettlement program called. They'd found a temporary job for me at the University of Vermont hospital. A woman who worked there was out on sick-leave and they needed someone to clean. I was happy to do whatever work I could find. They paid $8.50 an hour.

My first day at work Linda Miller drove me to the hospital in the morning. I took my bike along in the car so I could ride back home in the afternoon. The city was still new and I didn't yet know the streets well so I tried to pay attention to the directions and streets to the hospital. It wasn't very far. About a mile and half. A ten-minute bike ride at most.

I worked that first day cleaning and mopping rooms. By the time I was done, it was three in the afternoon. I stepped outside with my bike and saw it was snowing. Everything looked different covered in white. I started on the bike. The roads were slippery. I pedaled one way but didn't recognize the road. So I turned around and went the opposite way. I looked for something familiar. I rode down another street. I stopped to ask someone directions but they didn't understand me. I got on the bike again and went down a long hill and ended up all the way down by the lake which I knew was wrong. It was snowing harder now. Cars kept going past and splashing wet snow. I begin to panic a little.

I started up the hill again. It was getting dark. I was wet and shivering and my heart was racing. I didn't know anyone and no one stopped. I didn't know where I was. I saw a police car and thought of asking but was afraid to ask. Maybe I'd get into trouble or not know what to say? So I kept going up the hill looking for the right road. It was after five o'clock now and dark, and I was freezing and sweating. At a corner traffic light, I stopped and asked a guy where Intervale was. He seemed to understand right away that I was new and lost and in trouble. He walked me a block away then showed me where North Street and Intervale was. I had passed that corner several times earlier but hadn't recognized it. That's Intervale? I asked. The guy said yes, it was.

When I finally found our house a few minutes later and Amina opened the door, I was so thankful.

She looked at me and said, You got lost didn't you?

I was never so happy to see her face.

If those first weeks in Vermont were hard, they were nothing compared to what we'd been through before. To tell you about those years I have to go back to the place where I grew up along the lower Juba River in Southern Somalia, a small town called Makalangow, a beautiful village where my family had farmed for five or six generations. We owned land there and a house and compound along the Juba River. My father had two wives, and with my mother and stepmother we were ten siblings. We all lived in the same compound composed of five houses made of mud with metal roofs and a separate building we used as a kitchen, the whole compound closed in by a fence and metal gates. My father owned a store where he sold our fruits and vegetables. We had two farms, one in Bandar Salama, the other in Kimitryea. Our farms were like gardens, with a mix of trees and row crops. We grew everything: onions, tomatoes. Garlic. Squash. Corn. Sesame plants for the seeds and oil. We grew amaranth for the grain but mostly the young leaves, which taste like spinach. We grew beans. Mung beans, adzuki beans. Okra and watermelon and all kinds of gourds. Guavas and papayas, coconuts, too. And, of course, bananas.

Our house and store and my school were in the village of Makalangow, but our farms were a few kilometers away, one up-river, the other down. So I spent a lot of time walking along the river to one or the other. Sometimes I spent the night out in the fields with one of my older brothers. I was closest to my oldest brother Abdulkadir. I spent all my time with him at home and on the farm but when he turned eighteen he got married and wasn't around as much and I ended up hanging out a lot with Mahdi, the second oldest. We didn't distinguish much between siblings and half-siblings; we were all brothers and sisters. Mahdi was my step-mom's son. He was a big joker, always playing practical jokes.

We spent hours together on the farm, moving the generator around to water the plants from the river. Sometimes we swam in the river and often we fished. When we worked in the field, we set up fishing line and traps and caught fish all the time. We caught catfish. *Sharab. Lubee.* A blackfish called *mellie maday*. Another kind called *kai kai* and *misherafeeto*—but catfish was our favorite. It was said that eating catfish was a good cure for malaria.

The river came from Ethiopia and went past our farm and continued east to Kismayo where it ended in the Indian Ocean. The best time to fish was right after the rainy season, the *gu*, when the river shrank a little and the water didn't run so fast. We used to bait a wire trap, a *macaadin*, with frog legs, and leave the baited trap overnight. Once, right after the rainy season, we caught the largest catfish we'd ever seen. A gray-and-white monster. He'd gotten stuck and struggled overnight and when we found him in the morning, he was already dead. He was so large we couldn't lift the trap from the river. I was with Mahdi, and we both struggled for a long time to lift the trap from the water. We had to cut the catfish in pieces just to carry him all home. My mother ended up making a great big stew with vegetables, but we also salted pieces and dried them on the metal roof of our house, preserving the fish. It was delicious for months afterward. Like all the food we ate and sold, you'd call it local and organic and very healthy.

There were many animals who lived near the farm. Many birds and reptiles. Crocodiles in the river. Hippos in the surrounding forest. Lions and deer and giraffe further in the forest—they never came near the farm. The only animals who caused trouble were wild boar. They'd come when our corn was ripe, a group of boar, ten or 20 at a time. It was always 65 to 70 days after we planted the corn. They knew or could smell when the kernels were turning sweet. We had to keep vigilant then. Sometimes I slept overnight in the field with one of my brothers. The boars would come at night, the largest one leading the way. We had built pit traps. When the leader fell into the trap he'd scream and the rest would scatter. After that they wouldn't come back that year, but maybe return the next to try again. The boar were just pests. Because we are Muslim, we'd never consider eating the wild boar.

Most of the people who lived in Makalangow were, like us, Somali Bantu. Somali Bantu look a little different than ethnic Somalis. We speak a different language, although Maay Maay and Af Somali are somewhat similar. We came to Southern Somalia centuries ago and settled along the Juba and Shebelle Rivers. Some Somali Bantu came as migrants from other parts of Africa, sub-Saharan or West Africa. Others were enslaved by Arabs and brought to East Africa to work. Unlike Somali pastoralists, who herd camels and are sometimes nomadic, we Somali Bantu traditionally cultivated the land. We are farmers. We know the earth. And though there are millions of us we've always been a minority in Somalia and have always faced prejudice and discrimination. In Somalia we were denied the full rights of "regular" ethnic Somalis. We were not allowed to hold government jobs, for example, or join Parliament. When the government needed us to help fight their wars in Ethiopia, we served honorably and didn't desert but still they didn't want us to marry their daughters or get the good jobs. In 1980, the military dictatorship of Siad Barre confiscated our lands and gave it to ethnic Somalis. They were trying to "settle" the nomadic Somali people with a program they called *Iskaschito.* They gave our land to camel herders. But what did camel herders know about farming? Nothing. The plan failed. The land they stole from my family filled with weeds and started turning back into forest. For five years my father fought the government to get his land back. I was six or seven years old when we gained ownership again of the land and started to heal the fields once more.

In general, though, life was good in Makalangow. We got along with all our neighbors, Somali and Somali Bantu alike. My father's farms did well. My older brother sometimes rented a truck and drove our produce to other towns. The only time I ever left Makalangow and felt uneasy was when I had to complete my compulsory military training. At 15 years old I traveled with my schoolmates down the Juba to Jamaame. We spent two weeks there training. Those two weeks were the longest of my life until that point. I missed home. I missed my family and the fields. Everyone hated the military government and its leader, President Siad Barre. People had been trying to overthrow him for years, which is why he needed more and more young men to fight for him. I suppose that's why they were training us at 15 years old.

When Siad Barre was overthrown by the rebels on January 26, 1991, I was 19 years old. Honestly, it is not easy to talk about what happened at that time when our world turned upside down. We'd been living peacefully in our village. I'd been going to school, learning the Koran. I played a lot of soccer. I worked on the farm. Everyone welcomed the news about the rebellion at first. Nothing happened in our village right away. The capital was far away. The president went into hiding. The rebels ran after him. Soon the situation got worse. People started killing and looting. It began in the capital. Then Siad Barre and his army fled Mogadishu, south toward Kenya. On their way they passed through the Juba valley and gave weapons and vehicles to his supporters in the Darood clan. That's when things got bad for the Somali Bantu and for our village. Unlike other Somalis, we weren't given guns or vehicles. We had nothing to fight with. We were sitting ducks on our farms.

When the fighting spread to our region, the militias came with their new weapons and killed people. They raped women. They looted homes and stores. No one was safe. One day that February we were working on the farm in Bandar Salama. I normally would be working with my brother Mahdi but he was sick that morning and stayed at home. So Abdulkadir came out instead to work with me that day. It was a Thursday. We were quitting work early because it was the start of the weekend, which begins Thursday nights in Muslim countries. It must have been around two or three in the afternoon. It's too hard to remember now. I can't tell you the specifics. Only that we were attacked on our way leaving the farm. We were both unarmed. They shot Abdulkadir. They killed him right in front of me. I ran. That's all I knew at the time. But they were attacking the whole village of Makalangow, looting and raping. I didn't fully know it then, but others were running too. Where was my family? Had they been killed, too? I had no idea then. All I knew was that they had shot Abdulkadir in front of me and they would shoot me too if I didn't run.

Later I found others who were fleeing Makalangow. Some I recognized. Others I'd never seen before. We started walking through the forest together away from the fighting and gunfire. We didn't know where we were going at first. It was a very hard time. For days we just moved one place to another, always walking.

There was an old man with us who'd been to Kenya before and knew a little about the landscape and where the border was, and we decided it would be safer there. So we started walking west toward Kenya. We didn't know how far it was or how we'd get there, but we kept walking. We rested when we grew tired then started walking again. And this went on for days, then weeks. We had no food. We had nothing to drink. People got sick and died along the way. Sometimes we had to eat dead animals. Other times we were attacked by animals. One person was killed by a lion. Others dropped from hunger or exhaustion. It was really terrible. We would walk each day until noon, then rest under a tree, then start again in the late afternoon.

It took 20 days to reach the border. We crossed into Kenya at Dobley. The UNHCR was set up there by the border and gave us food and water. Eventually we were put on a bus then driven about 50 miles away to a big makeshift camp in the middle of nowhere.

Dadaab was out in the open with a big fence around it. We were relieved to be there alive at first. It was as if we'd escaped a fire and survived the flames and there were other people who had survived, too, and all of a sudden we weren't on fire anymore and could breathe for the first time. It was a relief not to be inside the fire. It was good to be able to breathe.

I found some people from my village in Dadaab. I tried to find information about my family. No one had any news. I feared others had been killed like my brother. How many and who I wouldn't learn for years.

Things in Dadaab started okay. The UNHCR gave us each a ration card. They handed out food. I even found a job. I was young and still strong from all the farm work, and I was picked out of a group because of my muscles. I dug latrines with a shovel. I earned 750 Kenya shillings a month. I was lucky to get the job because most people had none.

But things quickly turned bad in Dadaab. The camp was close to the Somali border. Men with guns would cross the border and attack us. They were targeting Somali Bantu. They'd come in the night when the camp police were gone. They'd jump the fence. When you left the camp to get firewood to cook with, you'd be attacked outside the fence. Women were raped. Children killed. It turned out that people inside the camp, non–Somali Bantu, were collaborating with those outside. The police didn't care. Each morning they arrived and simply recorded whoever was killed or raped the night before. We were powerless once again. We had nothing to fight them with. It was a genocide happening to us both in Somalia and there in Dadaab, a place where we were supposed to be safe. I saw my neighbors get killed. We had nowhere to go. Every day was another trauma.

The officials at the UNHCR slowly realized the problem. They started transferring Somali Bantu people to a safer camp further away from Somalia on the other side of the country. I didn't wait around but left the camp on my own with a cousin. We hitchhiked away from Dadaab. We found a lorry that took us to Garissa, then another truck that drove us south to Garsen. We had no papers. No identification. It was a little dangerous but nothing compared to what we'd been through. Because we looked more like Kenyans than Somali people, no one stopped us at the checkpoints. No one asked for ID. From Garsen we took a bus to Malindi, then another bus to Marafa where we arrived at the new camp.

Marafa was not far from Malindi, a beautiful city on the Indian Ocean, and Mombasa was a two-hour drive away. Things were immediately better in Marafa. No one was targeting us. The camp was safe, the ocean nice. The Giriama people who lived in that region were welcoming. Our cultures were similar. They even loaned us plots of land where we could grow our own food. At the camp, the UNHCR dug a well, provided water and food. Families were given tents to live in. I was alone at the time so they only gave me a piece of plastic and a tarp to use for shelter. But it was okay; there was enough space, and with poles and the tarp I made a shelter even though it was hot during the day.

I still didn't know what had happened to my family, but in Marafa I met people from Makalangow. My father's cousin was there. So was a girl I remembered from the village. I used to see her outside her house in Makalangow when I walked to the farm in the mornings. Her parents had a farm and they were distantly related to mine. Amina was very young when the war broke out, but now in the camp when we met again she was a little older. I reunited with her family. They took pity on me because I was all alone. Her father was very kind and invited me to eat meals with their family. He knew that my own father was missing and one of my brothers dead. So he took me in. I became almost like a son to him.

It wasn't long before I asked Amina and her father if I could marry her. Her father accepted and Amina accepted and we were happy. We had a typical Islamic wedding in Marafa. We sat and signed papers. I agreed that Amina was now my wife and I would take care of her. We had a big party that lasted all day and into the night, with music and dancing, the women in one place, the men in another. I was 24 years old, Amina 17.

I built us a small house with sticks and wood and a plastic tarp for the roof and thatched the top with grass to keep the inside cool. This was partly how we built houses back in Somalia, with a kind of woven grass called *ess*. Inside we had a *burgico*, a small stove. We cooked everything on it with wood we gathered in the forest outside the camp. I started growing vegetables again on a little plot of land loaned to us by our Giriama neighbors. Beans and corn and potatoes, providing for us and other families. The UNHCR gave us flour and maize and salt. Sometimes rice or pasta. Occasionally tins of sardines. Sometimes Arab agencies gave us food or clothing.

My father's cousin lent me money then to start a business. With 400 shillings I'd take the two-hour bus into Mombasa, purchase fruit and vegetables at the market, and haul them back to Marafa, where I sold them in the camp. The Kenyan currency was strong at that time so I'd make a small profit. The camp was good. There was enough food. I was growing crops again; I even paid people to work for me. We lived for a while without tension between the people inside and outside. I was starting to enjoy life with Amina. Marafa wasn't home, but it felt as close to home as anything since leaving Somalia.

We lived in Marafa from 1993 to 1996. These were mostly happy years. Amina got pregnant and our first son Abdihamid was born. Yet just when things seemed okay, the Kenyan government announced they were going to shut down Marafa. At the same time our son got sick with malaria. It was a big blow. We gave him medicine the camp doctor provided but it didn't help. He lived less than a year before he died.

The UNHCR moved us then to another camp closer to Mombasa. Utanga was only seven kilometers from the city. We were given no rations there, no food. So people had to look for whatever work they could find. Women took in laundry and washed clothes. Some people worked in Mombasa. We did any kind of work to survive. I started going to the market in Mombasa. Instead of selling fruits and vegetables, which were easy to get now in Utanga, I bought bundles of qat. Qat is a plant, a shrub, grown in East Africa. People all over the region chew fresh qat leaves because it is a stimulant and gives you a buzz. Qat is legal in Kenya, and grown around Mombasa by the Meru people, who are ethnically Bantu people. So I started going to the Kongoweah Market in Mombasa and buying bundles of fresh qat and bringing them back to Utanga to sell. I made good money at it, 400 or 500 shillings each time, which was about eight to ten dollars. But qat is addictive. You sit around and chew the leaves and become a little happy and numb. I was selling the leaves to other refugees. But soon I started chewing it myself. I would stay at the Kongoweah market until midnight or after, chewing qat with friends. It was hard to resist. The truth is: I was becoming an addict.

Our daughter Safia was born around then in Utanga. She too came down with malaria. But we were lucky and she survived. We had another daughter then named Lul, who sadly died from malaria. When our fourth child Haji was born, he, too, got malaria. You could go to the UNHCR doctors at Utanga but there was always a huge crowd waiting outside. You'd show up at six in the morning and wait until noon in the hot sun. People would literally just drop dead while waiting on line to see the one doctor. But if you had your own money you could see a private doctor. Since I was making money now from selling qat I was able to afford this time a private doctor who lived inside the camp. The private doctors were also Somali refugees who'd fled the country. They were knowledgeable and trustworthy and practiced modern medicine, not traditional medicine (which sometimes made the problems worse). Fortunately, with the medicine, Haji survived.

We buried Lul outside the camp.

We started to put together a life in Utanga. But one year after being forced there from Marafa, we were told we had to move again. They were now closing Utanga. We had to relocate. This time back to the place we first had to flee from: Dadaab.

Imagine how it feels to be forced from one place to another within a few months or years. To be forced back to a place you know is unsafe. Dadaab was a death sentence for Somali Bantu. We could only conclude they were trying to kill us all.

We organized. We formed a group of Somali Bantu. In August of 1997 we made the long journey to the capital, Nairobi. We went there to protest, me and Amina and Safia, our only child at the time. We traveled to Nairobi with everything we owned on a bus loaded with others, my brother and wife, too. We got off in in front of the United Nations office in the middle of the city and there, along with hundreds of other Somali Bantu in the same situation, we protested about having to return to Dadaab. We camped outside the UNHCR office. We didn't want to get anyone in trouble, but we needed to get our message out to the world, to let people know we'd be killed if sent back to Dadaab. For two nights we camped on the street outside the UN office. The government, the police, the UNHCR didn't want us there. On the third day the government and the UNHCR agreed not to send us back to Dadaab. They brought in buses. They decided they'd transfer us way out to western Kenya near Uganda to a camp called Kakuma. Kakuma was also dangerous but not as bad as Dadaab. The bandits there who came into the camp and attacked people at least attacked *everyone*, Somali Bantu and non-Somali Bantu alike. They didn't care about who they attacked as long as they had a little money.

We left Nairobi in the late afternoon. They put us in an overcrowded bus. We stopped late at night and slept in Kitali, then started the next morning and drove throughout the day. We arrived in Kakuma at sunset. There was nothing there but a hot dusty landscape and a fence that closed in thousands of people. No trees. Nowhere to plant anything. No town or city. Kakuma was in the middle of the middle of nowhere. Even its name—Kakuma—meant "nowhere" in Swahili.

We settled in as best we could. It was August and incredibly hot, even in the evening. Kakuma was a huge camp that had been set up originally for refugees from Sudan. It had grown over the years and now there was Kakuma 1 and Kakuma 2 and 3, an enormous place with rows of tents in the middle of nowhere. The UNHCR had an office there and the International Organization of Migrants and dozens of other organizations. By then, the UNHCR and the American government had begun to realize the special needs of Somali Bantus, how we were facing genocide inside Somalia and in the camps. So we'd been given priority as a stateless people and that gave us a glimmer of hope.

In Kakuma we applied for a B2 Visa to the United States. In 1999, the US embassy in Nairobi accepted our family's application. That began the long process of pre-screening and screening by the United States Immigration Service, a process that went on for five years. We were questioned and interviewed for years, by the JVA, by the INS. We were asked every kind of question, about our life, what we'd been through, how many people attacked us. Who was raped. Who was tortured. How many killed. All types of questions. The INS people asked you about things you said to the JVA people. They repeated things back to you to catch you up, to make sure you weren't lying. Then there were the medical examinations. Were we healthy enough? Did we have any problems? When we passed the pre-screening and the screening and the medical—that's when the long wait began.

There was a large wooden board in the Kakuma 2 part of the camp where the UNHCR and other organizations posted important notices. It was kind of a gathering spot for everyone in the camp. At two o'clock each afternoon, they posted lists of people who had meetings with immigration or medical or fingerprinting and people who had finally made it and were going to Nairobi to the office of the International Organization of Migrants. I spent so many afternoons in those years waiting at that big board with hundreds of others to see if our family's name appeared on the lists. So many months and years worrying that something would go wrong and we'd be rejected, that we'd be stuck in Kakuma forever.

During those years, I started taking adult education classes. I learned a little English. At some point Amina and I attended training and orientation where they taught us the culture of American people and their rules of what is allowed and not allowed. They taught us how to deal with people we've never met. We learned a lot of useful things, especially concerning gender. For in our community, in Somalia, it is not usual to see a woman who is a boss. So they taught us back then that we might have a woman who is our boss in America and that we had to be respectful. We couldn't just say, *I'm not going to listen because she is a woman.* We would have to adjust to the American way.

The people who taught orientation were mostly Somalis who'd lived in the United States. They came to Kenya to teach us but they didn't always explain everything. They left out important parts. Like the idea of paying rent for a place to live and having to pay for heat and electricity and taxes. They didn't tell us about this thing called a tax return. So when I came here I didn't know that if I made money, I would owe the government at the end of the year some of that money. No one ever explained it. That was a total surprise! On the other hand, they told us useless things like: You can't smoke outside in America. But then I saw people smoking outside the first few days after I arrived. They told us: You can't spit on the ground in America. But people spit on the ground all the time.

One thing I learned in orientation was that in America everyone has their own personal doctor. I thought that meant you were given your very own doctor. So when I got here and learned that doctors have hundreds of patients, it made me laugh. I thought that everyone literally had one doctor to themselves!

One afternoon in 2004, our name appeared on the big board in Kakuma 2. We were being called for fingerprinting. This meant we were close to actually leaving. About a week later, when I saw my name and Amina's and all our kids names listed on that board, saying we were due in Nairobi at the IOM office, I ran back to tell Amina. We were leaving Kakuma. We were going to America. That night I slept better than ever before.

Before we were assigned a place where we'd be sent in America, we had to sign a paper saying we'd pay our airfare. They pay for it up front, but you have to promise you'll pay it back in the future. Once I signed the papers, they told us where we'd be going. Vermont, they said. Colchester, they said. I was confused. I said, I thought we were going to the United States. Where is this Colchester? Where is this Vermont?

They assured me Vermont was part of the United States.

I must have looked doubtful.

Don't worry, they said. You're going to America.

Things then happened fast. In less than a week they took away our ration cards and destroyed them. They gave us the papers we needed. They took us to the Kakuma airfield in Kakuma town about three miles away. A small airplane flew us to Nairobi. There we waited in the IOM's accommodation center with hundreds of others. Mostly Somali Bantu from all over, some going to Australia, others Norway or Holland or, like us, to the United States. We were given our own bedroom. We were there for nine days with our group of 40 families heading to the US. We took more training classes. We couldn't leave the area. Then we were driven one afternoon by bus to the Kenyatta International Airport and we all got on a plane.

I've lived now in Burlington almost 20 years. Three of our babies were born in Vermont. It was a very different experience raising children here in the States, starting with things like diapers, which we never needed to buy before. We had to learn a lot. We had to adjust. I soon found another job working for an asbestos removal company. I started making more money. Eleven dollars an hour. The extra few dollars helped us pay for the gas and food and rent. Twenty years later, I still work for the same company today but now I am a supervisor. I took 40 hours of training in Springfield, Massachusetts. I got my certificate nine years ago. We get people working for us from Lowell, Massachusetts, Latinx people mostly, and we show them how to do the job. The company and my bosses are nice to me, and I'm nice to them. I remember back in Kenya during orientation they told us we might have a woman boss and I'd have to get used to that. I didn't think much of it at the time. The funny thing is, since I came here, all my bosses have been women!

My family is now scattered. Both my older brothers died when the war started. Abdulkadir, shot in front of me, and Mahdi, who was sick that day and didn't come to the farm, was killed later along with my stepmom. I didn't get to bury any of them.

In 2000, nine years after last seeing her, I found out my mother was alive in Kenya. I'd been writing to the International Refugee Committee, who deal with displaced or disappeared people, and after some time they located her. We started writing to one another once I found her. I asked her a lot of questions. We reunited in 2001. She told me when the war broke out, she fled with one of my my sisters south, to Kismayo, where she had relatives. My father fled north to his people's village. He went missing for a long time but ended up back in our village and died there a few years ago. My brother Abass was resettled to Phoenix, Arizona. My sister Safia was resettled in Seattle, Washington, but moved to Phoenix to be near Abass. My mother herself got resettled to Saint Louis, Missouri, then moved to Seattle to be with my sister before they both moved to Phoenix to all be together with Abass.

Two of my sisters still live in Dadaab. They want to come to America but don't have approval from the US embassy. Over 500,000 others are in the same situation, so they have little chance of coming here. It's not safe enough for them to go back to Somalia.

One of my sisters, Lul Mohamed, lives in Utica, New York. My youngest brother Abdihamid moved to Phoenix to be with the family. Another brother is in Somalia near Makalangow. I call him sometimes. I support him. I send him $100 from time to time. He is back on the family land in Bandar Salam and some of it he cultivates. I'm still friends with some of the Giriama people we knew when we lived in Kenya, though they've all grown quite old. I talk to them sometimes on the phone.

Our own kids are: Safia, Haji, Fardumo, and Gemana. Mahdi, who was born here; then Aisha and Abdulrahman. Safia went for four years to the University of New Hampshire. She is very smart and wanted to be doctor, then a lawyer. She ended up being a high school teacher who teaches kids now in Winooski. She has three children of her own and I am a grandfather! Haji goes to Champlain College in Burlington. Fardumo went to Haverford University and is now in Denmark studying medicine. Gemana and Aisha are both in high school. Mahdi is in the middle school and Abdulrahman in primary school.

I like it here in Vermont, yet I would also like to go back and see my beautiful village one day and enjoy the life we used to have back then on our family's land.

The problem is how to travel there and be safe. Militiamen and terrorists now control the area. Al Shabab is there. They invite and welcome all the criminals from Afghanistan and Egypt. I'd love to go back and see Makalangow but the war is endless and there is sadness all around. I was 20 years old when I was forced to leave and now I'm a grandfather and the situation is the same.

In my marriage, Amina and I are a team. Whatever decision I make I do so with her. She knows everything and we consult together, and our children see us working together as a team. If the parents have a good working relationship, the kids will have good relationships. If there is understanding in the parents, there will be understanding in the children. But if the mother is doing one thing and the father the other, that's a problem. Even when we have a disagreement, we don't talk about it in front of the kids. It's the culture I grew up with. If you teach your kids to respect people, they usually will. If you teach them how to treat people well, they will be fine. But if you treat them to disrespect others of different classes or castes, different races or cultures, than you create a problem.

I like teaching children now about Somalia, what the culture was like back then before the war, before colonization. I teach children but also people in their twenties who don't know much about Somalia.

I teach my kids that all humans are the same, whether Christian, Jew or Muslim, Black or White. Every human is to be respected.

One of the things I miss the most is being a farmer and growing food the way we used to in Makalangow, on our two parcels of land. I have a small plot now in a local community garden a few miles away in Colchester, Vermont. I spend time there in summer and fall and grow vegetables for the family. Cucumbers and gourds. Tomatoes. Corn. Things I used to grow in Somalia and some new things. The plot at Pine Island Community Garden is small, maybe 20 by 40 feet. Not the big lands I used to cultivate. It's a small thing but at least it's a way of putting down roots.

Fardusa

I was born in 1975 in the the small city of Bardera in Southern Somalia. I was the only daughter, with one older brother and one younger and me right in the middle. My dad drove a truck and delivered produce from our region sometimes as far as the capital, Mogadishu, which we called Xamar, which was about 500 kilometers away.

The name "Bardera" comes from the type of palm trees that grew in our area, yet the city was also called the "onion capital of the world" after all the fruit and vegetables that came from there. I grew up in a mud house with a thatched roof along the Juba River, but at some point my father built a new house of cement and stone, with a kitchen, a living room, a bathroom. We even had a room for a visiting guest.

Girls didn't go to school back then, so I had to stay at home and do the chores and learn how to cook and clean. And while most families were large, ours was small and I was the only daughter. So I had no sisters to share the work with. All the tasks fell to me. Making the bread—the canjeero—and the soup for breakfast, cooking the meat or liver or rice or pasta for lunch, and later in the day serving whatever was left from the morning soup.

Before I was ten, I learned all this, and how to clean and take care of the house while my older brother went to school. One of my biggest regrets was missing out on education. We grew up in a society where girls just didn't go to school. I didn't think much of it at the time. I never asked my family why. School was never even a possibility. But later on—and until this day—it affected and bothered me that I never learned to read or write as a child. At the very least, it hindered me in profound ways, which is why I was so determined that my own children get an education regardless of whether they were a boy or girl.

One place I did learn was at the movies. There was an old cinema in Bardera where they showed films imported from India. My friends and I would sneak into town and find a place outside the theatre where there was a hole in the wall and you could watch the film for free. We used to do this all the time. My father would sometimes catch me. If he was in a bad mood he might punish me—but often he just laughed, then asked about the movie. What was the story about? What was the music like? I'd tell him or sing to him the popular songs. Though, honestly, none of us understood a word of Hindi. Still, we enjoyed the musicals and would sing along and make up our own words and stories. And these were the stories I'd tell my father. The ones we made up. He always forgave me after.

On the day a new film arrived in town, a car would drive around the neighborhood with a loudspeaker attached to its roof and the driver inside would announce the name of the movie and the time it was playing that afternoon. When we heard the loudspeaker, the guy calling for the movie, all my friends would get ready. We didn't care what what the movie was, or what it was about. There was something always exciting about the cinema and a new film. We had live arts in Bardera too—a government theatre, with acting and dancing—but I loved the movies the best. They were so strange and magical. They brought us to places we'd never seen before. They showed us exotic things we didn't know. The first movie I ever saw was a famous Indian movie, already old at the time, Raj Kumar's *Nagin*. It was a story about this woman who took revenge on seven men who killed her husband. She did so by turning herself into a snake. The first time I saw it, it blew my mind. Everyone was talking about it. I was about 11, and the film was in Hindi and we just just followed the story. We didn't know or care about what they were saying. We picked up some Indian words. But it was seeing those people from India, the different dresses and culture and language that was so eye-opening, as was the plot: the woman's revenge, her killing the men, the snake.

After the movies, we'd often go for a snack in town. There was a small place that sold the hot sweet candy, halwa. I loved the old lady who made the halwa. She had a place where you could sit and eat the red halwa. Her name was Hawa. Hawa who made halwa. Then there was the *sambusa* guy named Sal, and the ice cream place. And there was always tea, inside or outside, red tea or sweet milk tea, *shah caddays*.

Because I was stuck at home with chores most of the day, my father brought me a radio. I lived for that radio, a National Panasonic. I listened to music, and if there was none, I refused to work. My father loved me. I was the only daughter. He'd do whatever I wanted. You could put a cassette into the Panasonic. The town only had electricity at night. But my father brought batteries for us to use during the day, which we'd take out at night when the electricity was turned on. The radio programs came from Mogadishu. The BBC from London. The news came in Somali. I listened mostly to music. Sometimes news or educational stuff for kids.

Like most young people, I was restless and eager to see the world outside our small city. I'd never been to the capital, Xamar. I wanted to go so bad because for me Mogadishu was like Paris or Mecca or New York City, a place I'd heard so much about my whole life. My father drove his truck there once a month. From Bardera he'd take onions or tobacco or melons and haul them to the city and come back with things from the city they needed in the rural area. Different trailers attached to his cabs, taking one thing here and another there. But I'd never been to Xamar and I'd never seen the ocean before. So I devised a plan.

I must have been nine or ten at the time and I had a cavity, a bad front tooth. In Bardera they couldn't do anything about it; there was no real dentist in town. Everyone went to Mogadishu if they had a big problem with their teeth or health. Because the problem with my tooth was not so bad, I decided to make it worse. That way, I'd get to go to the big city. I put a glass bead in my mouth and bit down where the cavity was. The bead got stuck in the hole in my gums and lodged there alongside the tooth. When I showed my parents, they were alarmed. They thought my tooth had turned black and decided they'd have to take me to Xamar. I'd have to go to a real dentist.

My father's truck had a a small bed in the back of the seat. I was so excited to drive to the city, to see the ocean, the big buildings, the markets. At the dentist's office, they found the glass bead. I had to confess to my father. He didn't get mad but laughed at the length I'd gone to to be taken to Xamar. They took out my bad tooth too, so it wasn't a complete lie. Afterwards, we went for ice cream and my father took me to the big cinema in the center of the town. The Cinema Equitore was so much grander than the one at home and we ended up watching two movies together, a Hindi movie and an American action film but I don't recall either of their names.

I never went to *dugsi,* religious school. Again, girls weren't supposed to back then. But I learned to pray from my mom, and my father taught me some suras from the Koran. When you pray you have to recite the suras so he taught me some of the shorter ones, which I memorized. I didn't know their meaning yet knew the words were religious and helpful to say. I learned even more from the other moms when we prayed together as we often did.

I have good memories of my childhood in Bardera, the warm embrace of the small city, the dusty streets, the red roofs, the palm trees along the river. It was a time I've never forgotten, the feeling of safety and family, the fruit trees, my aunts and uncles. Us kids were young and full of energy, and I was, to be honest, a bit of a troublemaker. My girlfriends and I would swim in the river, even though there were alligators and females weren't supposed to. If my parents were coming back, we'd rush into the house and pretend we hadn't been swimming. I'm not sure we fooled anyone.

The war changed everything. How much my parents knew beforehand, or anyone knew, I don't recall. Only that one day we kept hearing terrible things on the radio. People were trying to kill the President. Then it was suddenly not safe anywhere. We listened to the Panasonic National. Everyone was afraid. In the afternoon we started to hear shooting and explosions around town. We heard that gangs of men were going around Bardera targeting young people, killing the boys and taking the girls captive. Any girl older than 12 was taken and raped. The sun went down and night came. We didn't sleep. We stayed in our house. The gunfire got louder. Around three in the morning, before sunrise, we decided to escape. We took whatever we could and left the house.

Who were the people attacking us? The gangs, the militias, the soldiers. We didn't know them. They were Somalis but from some other place. It's hard to put together now. I was so young and have been through so much since. My father didn't own his truck so we had to go on foot, along with everyone else—neighbors, friends, people we didn't know. We walked into the bush. For ten hours we just walked. All through the night and into the next day. By the next afternoon we were in a dry place like a desert, a scrubland, where people kept camels and goats. Someone knew we'd be safe there. And it was true, the people welcomed us and gave us water and food. They fed us *soor,* a kind of corn porridge like polenta. They said we could stay in their area, and they helped us build huts. We stayed in that place for a few weeks, but then the war came there, too, the bad people with guns and trucks. It was Ramadan, I remember. They came in the dark, at the earliest part of morning, right before *Fajr,* four a.m. They caught us off-guard. We didn't have time to take anything but just ran. The first time when we fled our town we all went together, but now everyone just ran to save their life. It was chaos. They shot in the air. They shot at the people. They kidnapped a lot of girls. They captured my aunt. A lot of people got lost. My father and older brother were separated from us. I fled with my mother and younger brother and our grandparents. Later, on the road, we found my aunt. She'd been raped by the men—but was alive.

Somehow we made our way back to Bardera, but the city was destroyed. The houses and stores and farms. The people were all gone. There was nothing left. We couldn't find food or water. We knew my father and older brother would head to Xamar, where my other grandparents lived. So we decided to travel to the capital, too, along with hundreds of others. We walked along the roads. We just followed the others. Sometimes we got a ride for a few miles. Then a big dump truck came, full of people, and we managed to squeeze in back with all the others.

We went straight to my grandparents' house in Xamar. They lived near the ocean, by the port in a neighborhood called back then Bilaag al Arab. We stayed there for maybe a month but things weren't safe. The fighting was going on. People were killed. Then one day some armed men came into our house. My cousin Mohamed tried to stop them. They shot and killed him. We ran from the house to the water. To the port. To the place where people had been gathering to escape. We had nowhere else to go. We'd tried everywhere on land and now we had to run to the sea.

But when we got to the port we saw thousands of people. They were all over the dock and the beach, people like us trying to flee the city.

There was one big boat in the port and people were pushing and you had
to push through the crowd. It was crazy. People were fighting to get on
board. In the crush we lost my grandparents but me and my mom and
younger brother got on. The boat was meant for livestock, for camels and
cows and goats. There were pens for chickens. The whole place stank of
manure and urine. No one cared. Everyone just pushed on to save their
life. People went down to a lower level, then a second middle level. A
third level up top. We were lucky. We ended up in the middle level, which
may have saved our lives.

The boat was heading to Yemen. It was the closest, safest place for boats
to go. The port of Aden was about a thousand miles from Mogadishu. My
father and older brother had left a few days before on an earlier boat, but at
that point we didn't know if they'd made it or where my grandparents were.

I don't remember much of the crossing. We sailed through the night
along the coast, then across the Gulf of Aden. The sun came up the next
day as we were nearing Yemen. I don't remember if it was before we got
off, or when we were getting off that we learned of the horror. People had
suffocated below, on the first level, in the bottom of the boat, where there
was no air or water. A lot of them died overnight.

When we reached the dock there was a crush to get off the boat. People
didn't know what to do. They just pushed again to get on land. There were
men in uniform shouting at us, but we didn't understand what they were
saying. We didn't speak Arabic, and neither did most of the others. The
police or soldiers were just doing their job, asking questions, but people
were afraid. A few among us spoke some Arabic and translated for the
rest. But others were so frightened they just started running the moment
they got off the boat. They found out later this was not a good move. But
you couldn't blame them. They were scared and people were shouting
and there were dead people in the bottom of the boat.

We were brought into a big warehouse by the port. It turned out to
be an ice factory, which was a good thing, given how hot it was at the
port in Aden. They let us stay in the ice factory, so we wouldn't die in the
heat. They brought us food and drink, enough to give us until they found
out what they could do. There were maybe two hundred of us and many
guards. There were no beds. People just lay down on the ground to sleep.

We stayed there for about a day. A distant cousin of my mother's lived in
Aden, and somehow she knew we had arrived. She came to the ice factory

to get us out. She had to give them some kind of proof to vouch for us. We did it all officially, which turned out to be the best thing we could have done. Because later we'd need official papers to live and work there. To go to the hospital, to bring the kids to school. This cousin took us and another family to her home in Aden where we stayed for two weeks. In the meantime she helped us locate my father and brother and my grandparents. They'd all made it safely to Sana'a, the capital of Yemen, in the north. Sana'a was about about a nine-hour drive from Aden. We decided to take a bus. We were happy and nervous as our cousin put us on the bus to the capital.

Outside of the movies, Yemen was the first foreign country I'd ever seen, the first place where people spoke a different language and had a different culture. Everything seemed strange at first. The way people dressed and spoke. The mountains were beautiful and jagged, and the roads clean and perfect. The buildings and houses were different from anything I'd seen in Somalia. Back home in Bardera there was not much infrastructure, and though Mogadishu had larger buildings and more people, it was not particularly modern. But what I saw those first few days in Yemen amazed me. Sana'a was a beautiful old city, the oldest city in the world. It had strange Arabic-style architecture, the very old, and the very new, modern buildings with clean paved roads. To me it seemed like the richest country in the world, with shiny new cars and trucks on the highways. And though I was still a little frightened, I loved everything I saw.

We reunited with my father and brother in an apartment in Sana'a Old City. They were with my mom's mom and father, who'd we lost at the dock in Mogadishu. All the Yemenis we met were nice and helpful. Neighbors came to the apartment and introduced themselves. They asked if we needed anything. Food or drink. They were really good people, always asking how we were and what we needed. That began our new life of exile in Yemen. It took a long time to get used to everything. The new language, the culture, the streets.

The big city was scary to me at first. Whenever I had to leave the apartment, I was terrified of getting lost. The streets were a big maze and I would panic, afraid I wouldn't be able to ask anyone how to get home. In time I realized there were plenty of other Somalis around who I could ask. You could actually hear Somali language in the street a lot of the time.

Back home we always cooked with wood. We'd have to gather the wood and make a fire. But in the apartment in Sana'a we had a gas stove, and this was remarkable and made it easy to cook. Back home we'd have to gather the water from a pump and carry it back in cans. But in Yemen the water ran out of a tap. Just like that: water! And the shower, that was beyond imagining. All that modern stuff, I admit, was very exciting for me at the time.

My father looked for a job. He started working in construction. Eventually he found work operating heavy equipment. He made concrete and crushed rock and drove a cement truck. My older brother, who was always obsessed with cars, found a job working with heavy machinery, too, big trucks, back hoes and excavators. Soon they were working together, father and son. I was around 16 at the time. I'd grown up so much in those few years since we were forced to leave our home in Bardera. All the things we'd been through made me grow up fast and appreciate life and being alive. I understood, when we found ourselves in Yemen, we had a second chance, so I seized on whatever opportunity I could find. At 16 I already knew life was a struggle, that nothing was assured, that things could be taken away just like that. I wanted to do so much. At home I still cooked and cleaned and took care of my mom and dad and brothers. But I also learned to work with fabric and beads—I was always good with cloth and crafts. Whenever I had free time I asked my mom to buy cheap hijabs from the store. I'd take the drab hijabs and embroider them with colorful beads in the shapes of flowers. I'd accessorize them. I could turn something inexpensive into something special and make a little money with my designs. I was a quick learner; people always said that. Even today people they say it. Fardusa, if you set your mind to something and try—two or three times, mashallah, I can figure it out. Back then I'd seen someone do the beadwork and figured it out myself. Soon my mom was buying fabrics and beads, then selling my designs to the woman who had a stall in the souk. The woman started taking orders for my work. I did the piecework at home. It wasn't a lot of money—but at least it was something.

Those years weren't easy. We had to adjust to many things. Back home in Bardera, we owned a house and land, and never had to think about things like paying rent or paying for water or wood. We took the sunlight and the air and water for granted. But in Sana'a we suddenly had to pay for everything, to live in an apartment and cook on a stove and use electricity, even for water to drink. And though my father and brother had jobs—and I'd make some change from my hijabs—we never had enough money to last the month. It was week to week with us, as it was for so many others we knew.

The culture in Yemen was much more strict and religious than it had been back home, especially when it came to women. Once I reached puberty, I could never go out in the street alone. I always had to be accompanied by a man. When I came to Yemen, I was just becoming a woman, which complicated an already complicated situation. Back home in Somalia, I was carefree and still a girl and could go everywhere and play with friends and it wasn't a big deal. But in Yemen I was suddenly a woman. A teenager, but a woman, who had to cover my face and hair and do it the way the Yemeni women did—covering my whole hands and feet and wearing a *burkha* with the long black veil over my face so only the eye slits were visible. In Yemen it's called a *baqa*. We never wore them back home in Somalia. So for me, it was really two big changes: becoming a woman and moving to a new country. Which meant in Yemen I had to stay indoors all the time inside the apartment. I could only go outside with my father. On top of that, I knew it would be like this until someone asked me to marry.

There'd been a boy on the boat that brought us from Mogadishu to Yemen. Like us, his family had fled Somalia and had settled in Sana'a. The boy had been injured the first days of the war in Mogadishu. I didn't know the whole story at the time but later learned that Ali had been sitting outside on the street when he'd been struck by a bullet. He didn't die. The bullet lodged in his back and partially disabled him but he was able to get around.

I remembered him from the boat, how we'd helped one another. Our fathers knew each other in Sana'a. So when I turned 18, Ali's father met with my father and they agreed we'd get married. The fathers shook hands. They read the first chapter of the Koran, the al-fatiha. They picked the date for the wedding.

Ours started in the afternoon with a sacrifice, and goat for lunch. All the families came, all the neighbors. The men went to one place and played music and chewed qat, while we women gathered in another place. I wore white and stayed with the females. Then, at the wedding, we danced to music. Then Ali came and picked me up and took me to his parents' house. It was 1994. I was 19 years old.

I moved across town to Ali's family's house in the more modern section of the city. His family lived in a small apartment in a four-story building off Beynoun Street in the southeast part of the city. It was a real shock to leave my home. I'd grown up in a small family, just me and my two brothers, and Ali, on the other hand, had a huge one. They were all crammed into a tiny apartment. Four families living together, Ali's three brothers and their wives and children, Ali's parents, and us. His oldest brother alone had five children and the second oldest had two and the third one wasn't yet married. The house was just one floor with three bedrooms and a small living room. One kitchen. One bathroom. Suddenly I was around all these people and had all these responsibilities. I had to clean and cook for the families—so many of them! It was a fulltime job and I was the new one without status. Ali was the youngest of four boys and four girls. Since he was the youngest, the older ones were already long married and had teenage or young adult children of their own. You can image how difficult that was for me, and the way they treated the young bride in their home, their "aunt" who was their own age. The moms were okay, at least they had compassion, but the nieces made my life miserable. The young ones were particularly bad.

Once, when I was pregnant with Mohammed, I fell on the stairs and clutched my stomach to protect my baby. I got banged up and hurt my leg. I couldn't walk, and was pregnant, but I still had to cook and clean, and the daughters made fun of me and teased me and made me get up and do things for them—even though they knew I was in pain. We had, what can I say, a complicated relationship. But it evened out in the end because as young women they were in the same situation I was in. Soon they would have to leave their mother's home and then they'd get their comeuppance. And when each went off to get married, the house opened up a little more, and my job became less demanding and the nieces had to fend for themselves. And soon those same nieces who'd tortured me came around to understand how hard it was to leave home and enter a new family. In this way the dynamic changed, and things got better between us. Age does that…and leaving home.

Mohammed, my first son, was born in 1995. I'd been in Yemen for four years by then and spoke a little Arabic. I learned mostly from the

TV. We had a black-and-white console with a dish on the building's roof. There were two channels in Yemen. North and South, each had their own programming. There were Yemeni shows and lots of Egyptian programs. That's how I learned Arabic, from Egyptian comedies. Adel Emam comedies were my favorite. We all loved watching him, the King of Egyptian comedy. We also watched a lot of dramas and films. Of course, I learned Arabic as well from other women in the neighborhood and just living in Sana'a.

Despite the bullet in Ali's back, he found a job as a bus driver. He'd wake up early in the morning before dawn and return late at night. He drove a bus in Sana'a from the new part of the city to the old, from Shumailah to Bebel Yemen, the Gate of Yemen, the historical entrance to the Old City. He went back and forth all day.

It was in those years I began to become my own person. I didn't have to ask for permission to do things. I decided to go to *dugsi*, which in Yemen is called *tafir*. I went with other women to learn about religion. My second baby Abdullah was born in 1997. Two rooms opened up in the house, so we had more room. The next year my third son, Abdulaziz, was born. After four months, we knew something wasn't right with him, the way he couldn't hold up his neck. We brought him to the doctor. They checked his bones. They checked his brain. They couldn't find anything abnormal. No one knew what was wrong. It may have been from a fall I endured while I was pregnant, or perhaps it was something else, but that's when things started getting difficult.

I got pregnant again in 2000 with Abbas, the fourth boy. By then Mohammad was five, Abdullah three, and Abdulaziz two. Having a baby with a disability was a big challenge. On top of that was the new baby, and the fact that Ali was angry because he really wanted a daughter and I kept giving him only boys. And this became a source of conflict and tension. We also didn't have enough money. Not with so many children, feeding them and paying the rent and buying drugs for Abdulaziz, and diapers for him, too, because he had no control of his legs and lower body. Even though Ali worked all day driving a bus, he was making only enough for our rent. We could hardly survive, and there was nothing like health insurance to pay for doctor visits or medicines, especially for a child with disabilities.

There was nothing I could do to relieve the stress. I had a feeling at that time of great heaviness, of constant strain. It was made worse by

Ali's wanting a daughter, and then my getting pregnant again. Zainab, our first daughter, was born in 2002, but we soon found out she, *too*, had a disability. She was slow at learning and not quite like other children, so that added another burden to the list. The challenges kept growing. Since I was able to give him a girl, Ali decided we should try again. In 2005 Hussein was born. Mashallah, he was a fine healthy baby. A year later, I got pregnant for the last time with our daughter Shirhan. But during that pregnancy, a bad thing happened. Ali lost his bus driving job. It was 2006. Jobs were impossible to find in Yemen at the time, so he did something unfortunate, based on bad advice. He snuck out of Yemen and crossed the border into Saudi Arabia illegally. He needed work and thought he could find a job there to help. But it was not a smart move. As far as I was concerned, he just disappeared. I was left alone, with seven kids, two with disabilities.

Objectively, the things that happened to me and my family in Somalia were difficult: the violence, the war, my aunt's rape, my cousin's murder. Yet I was still young at the time and surrounded by my family. The adults were responsible back then for figuring out what to do and how to take care of us. During the war there were just moments. A few intense moments when you got really scared and thought your life might end but then you lived through the moment and went on and had good moments again. That was war. That was running away. The good moments later help you forget the bad. The lows, the highs. But now, in Yemen, in the small apartment with all my babies and the disabilities and not hearing a word from Ali, I was all alone to figure out what to do. The challenges I'd experienced before were not easy, but what happened in Yemen, in Sana'a, was somehow harder, more cutting and enduring, the constant stress and challenge that had no end in sight.

With Ali gone I became, overnight, both the mom and the dad. I had to take care of the babies, discipline and teach the kids, and find work to get food for everyone. Food and diapers and medicine. I was still pregnant at the time when Ali left. I didn't hear from him for some time. No one knew what had happened to him. Where he was, or if he was even alive. I searched for him for a while, called everyone I knew. We had no phone back then. No house phone, no personal phone; it was hard to communicate. Years later I learned he was caught by the Saudis without papers and deported back, not to Yemen, but to Somalia—Shirhan was already three when we found out. But I didn't know this then and his disappearance added to all the other stresses.

The challenge now was in two parts: The older kids had to go to school, and the youngest and disabled ones still needed diapers and to be looked after. Because I had no schooling myself, I insisted the older ones, Mohammed and Abdullah, go to school, and that cost money. But I wouldn't compromise. No matter what, I was determined that they get an education. I lived through that. Whenever I worked, I separated money for kids for school and kids for different (special) needs—and house needs. It was too much for me to handle all these at the same time. Mom and dad and money-maker.

It was around this time a neighbor asked if I'd make *sambusas*. There was a small restaurant nearby that sold prepared food. Adnan's restaurant was a small place on a busy street near a private school that was always crowded with pedestrians and students. Adnan needed someone to help make *sambusas* and I agreed to make them at home where I could keep an eye on the children.

Sambusas are like Indian *samosas* but smaller. Little triangle pastries stuffed with savory meat or vegetables. Onions, potato, peas, beef or chicken. They're baked in an oven or deep fried. I'd learned how to make them from my mother, and somehow Adnan knew I could cook. So I made him 100 *sambusas* at first as a trial. People loved them. He sold out. He hired me to make 100 *sambusas* each day at home. He'd sell them at his restaurant and I'd get a percentage. But soon the word got out: they were popular. Then he wanted 500 a day!

To make *sambusas*, you have to make the dough the night before. You take flour and water and salt, then you rub oil into the flour with both your hands. You stretch and knead the dough then leave it covered to rise overnight. The next day you make the filling for the different types of *sambusas*. Then you roll out the dough in a circle and cut it into pieces, fill each piece and pinch and oil them shut and put them in the oven. It is a long, laborious process. And to make 500 of them takes some time.

But I did it. Alone at first, while watching the kids. When they came out of the oven, the *sambusas* smelled great to everyone—except me. After a week or two, I became sick of the odor!

The *sambusas* became my lifeline. I was making enough money to pay for rent and food. I also had my own delivery boys, Mohammed, Abdullah and Abbas. It was a ten-minute walk to Adnan's place, and they piled the *sambusas* on a tray under a dishtowel on top of their heads. Since we couldn't afford a taxi, they'd have to walk the whole way and deliver 500 of them to the restaurant. Though sometimes—and I didn't learn this until later—people would see them and smell the fresh *sambusas* and stop them and ask to buy a few, and the boys would sell a dozen before they even got to the restaurant.

I worked every day of the week. No days off. Seven days a week. I kept watch over the children. Some days after I made 500, the man would send his brother to ask me to make even more. So I asked a neighbor if she'd come to the house to help make the *sambusas*—it was just too much for one person. The neighbor and I started making them together, In the small kitchen, Abdulaziz in the baby's wheelchair where I'd watch him; the kids would play close by in the living room where there was no door.

By the time Shirhan turned five I was doing so many things. In the morning I worked in the school cafeteria. I left at 6AM, cleaned the cafeteria and made lunch for the school kids. In Yemen the schools closed at 1PM I'd come back home then and feed my own children, and then I'd start making the 500 *sambusas* from three until five or sometimes six. Every day was like that, except for two days break from school. When I was at work at the school cafeteria, my mom came over and stayed and watched the kids, and if she couldn't, my upstairs neighbor took care of them. They just needed someone to wake and feed them breakfast, and then the kids learned how to do it themselves. They used to wake up around ten or 11 and I'd almost be home by then. The school where I worked was a 15-minute drive away. Too far to walk. I had to take a taxi. The three older boys were in school.

My mom helped a lot back then. She still lived with the family back in the old part of the city. She'd come and stay with us for four or five days and help cook and clean and watch the kids. Then she'd go back to my father and brothers and not return for several days. But then something happened to the bottom half of her body. She couldn't walk or feel anything below her waist. We brought her to the hospital and they found a tumor on her spine. They said she needed surgery. We thought it might be cancer but when they did the surgery and cut the tumor out, they found it was benign. It weakened her spine, and after the surgery, she had to take medicine to make the bone and spine stronger. They said, "Give it nine months and you'll walk." But after nine months she could move only her toes. During those years, she stayed with my brothers all the time. Since I was the only daughter, I had to make time to visit her in the late afternoon, after finishing the *sambusas,* to check and stay with her for a few hours. I was taking care of both the old and the young. Those were tough years. But after two or three years, mashallah, she was able to get out of bed. She'd hold onto the wall while she moved around the house. It took her a long time to recover and walk again.

Sometime during those years my brother's wife was talking to a lady about me and my two kids with disabilities, how Abdulaziz was in a wheelchair and couldn't get around and Zainab had a developmental disability. The lady told her about an organization that helped families with disabled children, sometimes with money or by finding a doctor or surgery overseas. My brother encouraged me to check out the organization. Who knows, he said, maybe they can help Abdulaziz? I had tried to get Abdulaziz help when he was younger. I'd brought him to school, but no one would take him. Not in public school. And neither would anyone take Zainab. Only special schools would look after children like them, private schools that cost a lot of money we didn't have.

One day I took off from work and went with this lady, my sister-in-law's friend, to the office of the International Organization of Migrants. We took three buses to get there. I was nervous but hopeful. It was the first time I had asked for assistance from any government agency—and this one was international.

When we arrived, there were dozens of people outside the building trying to get in. Since the lady had made us an appointment, we were on their list, and the guard let us in. We met there with an Iraqi man. I showed him photographs of Abdulaziz and told him about our situation. He asked many questions and said many things and wrote down everything I said about the family and our past. At the end of the meeting, he said he was going to send our case to his managers and see if they could help. He seemed encouraging. He said to come back in one week. I didn't need an appointment, he'd put my name on a list.

I went back by myself the next week, but the Iraqi man said he had no news, come in another week. So the following week I returned once more.

This time he told me I qualified to get some help for Abdulaziz's needs. Aside from that, there was nothing they could do for him in Yemen. His needs were too great and they didn't have facilities for him there. So he'd sent our case to their international office of the IOM to see if an outside country would help us. It meant they were going to build a case for us overseas. This was a big deal. He thought we had a good case because we were refugees from Somalia to begin with.

Soon after, we began our official application for refugee status to whatever country could help us with Abdulaziz, any country that had modern facilities and health care. I had photographs taken of each of the children, with a white background, and brought them to the Iraqi man. We met at the IOM's international office, in a different building in another part of the city, where a foreign lady interviewed me. At the same time, I started to receive a little money each month from the local IOM office, money to help pay for food and medicine and diapers for Abdulaziz. The money wasn't much, but the support changed my life. For the first time I had enough food for the kids. I could take a taxi if I needed to. It was enough to get by. But not enough to stop making *sambusas* every day.

All this was happening around early 2008—the application, the new support, the waiting to hear from the IOM. I tried not to think about it too much. Life went on. Months passed, then a year passed, then two. At some point during that time the money from the local IOM stopped coming. I didn't understand why, but learned later that someone in our neighborhood found out about the support I was getting from the IOM and went to their office and lied about me. Probably because she was jealous. She said I was rich and that I was making up the story about Abdulaziz and that I owned my own house and didn't need any help!

I didn't even know at first about it, except they stopped calling me to come get my money each month. I didn't want to make any waves or upset anything that was happening on the international side. So I said nothing.

It was around this time when Mohammed, my oldest son, came home one day with money he'd earned from playing soccer. I didn't believe him at first. What teenager makes money in Yemen playing soccer? But Mohammed was telling the truth. The fact is, he was a very good soccer player, so good that one of the top private schools in Yemen offered to let him study at their school in exchange for him playing soccer. He also got picked by a semi-professional league and began playing for a soccer club and making a little money. Most kids in Yemen need money for soccer. To buy shoes or jerseys, but not Mohammed. He was very modest about it, coming home with money each month. The best part was that he was finally getting a real education. The public school he'd been going to was so crowded, he never even bothered going to class, because there were hundreds of kids in one class and they couldn't even hear the teacher and no one really learned a thing. But now he went to school with all the rich kids of the capital, wearing a uniform and actually learning other subjects, aside from just playing soccer. And, mashallah, he was helping the family with money.

So God took away from one side and gave on another side. With the money Mohammed made playing soccer, I didn't need to ask the local IOM office for support. I didn't want to say anything to to ruin the chance with the international side. I kept working. I laid low. I never found out who had gone to the organization and lied about us. Later, when someone from the IOM came to investigate, they found out I wasn't lying. We were not rich. We didn't own our apartment. We rented from someone who lived in Saudi Arabia. I bought my food on credit. My husband was missing. We didn't know where he was. I took care of all these children myself. Why should I lie? I wondered why they believed this other person in the first place? Why didn't they send someone sooner to find out I was telling the truth? I didn't bother asking. People just try to survive. I was fine. My kids were fine. Leave the bad with the bad. I was okay.

For two years we waited while our application went through. Once in a while I had to fill out some paperwork or meet with foreigners or go for an interview. Then one day, at the start of 2011, I got a phone call from the IOM saying they wanted the whole family to come to the Sheraton Hotel in Sana'a. They wanted us to meet with some Americans. The interview would take all day so they had gotten us a room at the hotel.

We were all very excited that day. We left before dawn to go across town to the Sheraton. We arrived at six in the morning. There were other families waiting for interviews, too, families similar to ours, with lots of kids, and one with some type of disability. They put us in a room with a couple of other families while we waited. Everyone had their own story. Because my kids were still minors at that point, they just checked on the children and then took me in for the interview. It lasted until the afternoon and then we went back home. We were all pretty enthusiastic. Because of Abdulaziz's disability, someone told us, we were probably on a priority list. Someone else said that if the Americans were already interviewing us in person, it meant we were probably already approved and that we should get ready, pack our bags. We could be moving to American any day!

When we got home, I called my parents and told them the news. They swore not to tell anyone, and the children all knew not to say a word. We were so happy that day. We were full of dreams.

It was the spring of 2011 then, what they later called the "Arab Spring." And it was exactly around then, or a few weeks later, when thousands of people started protesting in the streets of Sana'a. It happened so quickly, the mass protests, then the violence, the killing, the bombs. Just like in Somalia so many years earlier, we were suddenly caught in a civil war. The whole city shut down. Schools closed. The government offices. The international aid agencies. All the foreign groups who were going to help us—all the foreigners—they fled the country. The airports closed down. The Battle of Sana'a began. Just like that, our hopes for leaving were wiped away. We were stuck again in a war-torn city. Just when things were looking as if they might change.

From then on, we were on our own. In the months that followed I tried calling the IOM but no one picked up. Even during the war that summer and fall I went back each week to the office in hope of seeing someone who would know about our case. It was difficult to get there. The city was still partly shut down. I'd take the different buses and arrive there after two hours and find the building was still closed and no one was there. Once in a while, if there was a security guy out front, I'd ask him, and he'd send me away. But I'd wait there for a few hours anyhow, hoping to see a familiar face come or go, one of the people I'd met before.

In those day there was an encampment in front of the IOM building where homeless people had set up because they had nowhere else to stay. They, too, were waiting for news from the IOM. A lot of Somali people were camped out there. I often hung out with them and talked, because we were in a similar situation. But sometimes the police would come and chase us all away and try to close down the encampment. So I had to be careful. I didn't want to get arrested. I had my kids to take care of.

One time the police opened a water cannon on everyone and drove them away. It could get violent there. As soon as I sensed any danger, I'd leave.

Soon I stopped going. I gave up. It was too dangerous, and no one was helping. It was time to move on. The saddest part was having to tell the kids, especially Mohammed. Back then, Mohammed used to wait by the door of the building for me to return. Each time he'd ask, "What happened?" Sometimes he could see it on my face, but other times I just shook my head. This time I told him the bad new for the last time: We weren't going anywhere.

I went back to my job at the school cafeteria. It was around 2012. I started cooking and bringing food for the school children in the morning as well—they gave me the opportunity and I took it, cooking in the morning for the school, and in the afternoon making *sambusas*.

And soon it all seemed like a dream, like it had never happened, the IOM and the idea of leaving and finding help for Abdulaziz. I couldn't wait around and dream about something that wasn't going to happen. I needed to get on with our life and make money for the family. The war was going on, but Mohammed still played soccer for his club. Soccer was one of the few things that united both sides in the civil war. They were hoping they could find peace through soccer, and he was one of the young rising stars. Perhaps he could make a career of it if the war ever ended. Occasionally I would think about going back to the IOM office, but I lost hope, for three years.

One day in late spring of 2014, I was making *sambusas* in the kitchen when the phone rang—I had a cell phone by then. I could tell the call came from someplace else.

"Is this Fardusa?" the man asked.

I recognized his voice immediately. It was the Iraqi man from the IOM. I hadn't heard from him in four years.

"We've been looking for you," he said on the phone. He was calling about our case and wanted to see the whole family again.

I stood there that day, trying to concentrate and remember everything he said, because I still couldn't read or write anything down. I had to focus on the time and address and place. It takes a different part of your brain when you can't write, when you have to memorize everything 100 percent. It's a problem I still have, not being able to write things down. And this was the call I was waiting for for many, many years. I was so worked up and excited. We'd only get one chance.

The next morning I went to work as usual. I made the *sambusas* in the afternoon. When I was finished, I took a taxi to the IOM office instead of the bus—I had enough money now from the extra work. The building was open again. I went to the security guard and gave him my ID and case number. Right away, he let me in. In the office the Iraqi man said they'd been looking for us, that our application was complete and they just needed to do a few final things. I had thought our case was lost once they'd all left Sana'a. But they'd taken all their files with them and had been working on our application overseas. It just took all this extra time because of the war. But we were still on their list of approved families. Before I left, the Iraqi man said, "Make sure you take your phone with you everywhere because any day you'll be getting a phone call to set up a meeting."

I got a cab home that afternoon almost in tears. I thought, *Wait until I get home and tell Mohammed the news.* But that day, when I got out of the cab and walked to the building, Mohammed wasn't there. He was at soccer practice. I was bursting to tell someone the news. I didn't tell the other kids. I waited for Mohammed to get home. I counted the hours, the seconds. And when he finally arrived in the evening, I gathered all the kids in the kitchen and told them: We are going to the United States. I remember how happy we all were that day. The joy. But I didn't quite know it if was really true.

It was winter 2014. I thought we'd be leaving in a matter of weeks. There was so much to do. The days passed. I cooked *sambusas* every day. I watched the phone. I didn't tell anyone the news. I made sure the kids told no one. Based on what had happened with the jealous neighbor, it wasn't safe to tell anyone anything. The days stretched on. Then the weeks. Two weeks. Three weeks. The doubts came back. Maybe it was all make-believe? The call came on the fourth week. They wanted the whole family to come to the office the next day. We got ready in the morning. We all piled in a taxi and drove to a different office in another part of the city, an office that seemed newly built. They took my fingerprints and the fingerprints of all the kids. They questioned the older kids. They grilled

Mohammed. They asked about Ali, my husband. Where was he? What had happened to him? They said they could do nothing until they located and contacted him and got his permission.

We left that day unsure. I found a contact for Ali in Somalia, the phone number of a store near where he was living. I gave that number to the organization. They also wanted eight photographs of the kids. A couple of weeks passed. Then we had an appointment at the American embassy. This was a big step. A big deal. There they would interview us again and we'd all have to be examined by a doctor.

The date was set for the embassy. I was really worried about that date and having everything we needed and what the medical people would say about Abdulaziz. Could he fly? Were we all healthy enough? Mohammed was in his last year of high school. It turned out the day of our big meeting at the American embassy was the exact same day as his high school final exams. For the last few years, he'd been going to a private school for wealthy kids. They'd let him in for free because of his soccer skills. It was a big deal because the education was excellent, unlike at the public schools, and he'd become interested in his studies and liked his teachers. But that day he had to decide. He could either miss his tests and not get his high school diploma or miss the medical and not be able to be there for us or get his own medical exam. I relied on him so much. I didn't want to pressure him. He said he'd try to do both. He'd take his exam in the morning and meet us at the office in the afternoon. I didn't like the idea. But it was his decision to make.

In the morning he went off to school. I was incredibly stressed. No one knew about our situation. None of Mohammed's friends or teachers at school. We couldn't tell a soul. We had to be at the office in the afternoon for the medical. I waited by the door all morning. At one o'clock I gathered the whole family together and we waited by the door. At 1:30 he still wasn't home, so I called a cab and we all got in and drove to Mohammed's school. I was hoping we would find him on the way, walking home. The school was rather far away, so we drove along the streets looking for him. It was a very hot day, the sun glaring. We drove around for a long time but didn't find him. I was panicking. And then suddenly, there he was, jogging along the street on his way home. The cab driver honked and waved him down. Mohammed get in, the driver shouted. He looked up, surprised. He was out of breath and drenched in sweat. But he'd finished his exams.

We drove home so he could quickly change out of his school uniform.

We arrived at the American embassy on time. We had our papers. We went through the metal detectors. There were Americans working there and Yemenis and South Asians. We were taken first to see a doctor, a South Asian man. He seemed to be in a really bad mood. He was angry about something. I remember exchanging a look with Mohammed and thinking, *This is not good.* He was quick and gruff with us and took one look at Abdulaziz in his wheelchair and said, "He's not fit to travel on a plane. It is not possible."

My heart sank. *This is it,* I thought. I started to feel faint. I was hyperventilating. I could see Mohammed getting furious. They made us leave the room and wait outside in a hallway. I don't know how long we were out there but I felt physically sick. Then another man showed up, a foreigner, an Arab. We told him what had happened with the doctor and the Arab man shook his head. He looked upset, a little angry.

"Don't worry," he said and waved for all of us to follow. We had to go up some stairs. He helped us carry Abdulaziz up the steps in the wheelchair. I don't remember what happened, but Mohammed said the two guys had some kind of confrontation. The Indian doctor said, "I already told them he wouldn't pass the test. They can't get on the plane." But the Arab guy said, "I think he will pass the test and we're going to let them try. I put my word on it."

It went like that for a while. They had a back-and-forth, and finally the Indian doctor relented and let us go.

Mohammed was the first to be tested. They took him into a room and a different doctor did a thorough exam. Blood, heart, pulse, chest. Then he examined everyone else. Abdullah, Abbas, Zainab, Hussein, Shirhan. They saved me and Abdulaziz for last. They took Abdulaziz first. The doctor asked about his mental state, if he gets angry or has episodes. No, I explained, he doesn't get angry. It's only his spinal cord, he has nerve damage and his legs don't work. That's all that's wrong with him. They took his vitals: He was perfectly fine.

Finally it was my turn to be examined. By that point I was a nervous wreck—with all we'd been through to get there and then the fight with the Indian doctor. Everyone could see the terror on my face. My exhaustion and anxiety. The doctor said, "You're dehydrated and your heart is racing." Then he took my blood pressure and said, "It's off the charts. Go outside," he said. "Take a rest. Have a drink of water. Then come back."

So I left the room and went outside for a few minutes. Tried to compose myself. But when I went back inside my pulse and blood pressure were still too high. The doctor said, "Look, you're just nervous and stressed. Don't worry. If they've done all this already for you and your family, you've already checked out. I'm going to have a look at another family now. Go outside. Don't overthink things. When you come back, I'll check your vitals again and you'll be fine. Okay?"

"Yes," I said. I was close to tears.

I went outside, and we stood out there in the lobby for about 45 minutes. I tried to think of nothing and just breathe. When I went back into the exam room, just as the doctor said, I was fine.

Still, the doctors decided it was best that Abdulaziz see another doctor to doublecheck that he could endure the long flight. They made an appointment for the next day at the hospital. And at the hospital, a specialist said Abduulaziz was perfectly fine. He can fly for three days without rest. No problem.

They gave me some medicine to give to the kids to keep them healthy before the flight. A few days later or so, we were given our IDs back with the visas for the flight. They also gave us money. Fifty dollars for me. Fifty for Mohammed. Twenty-five for each of the other kids to go shopping to buy stuff before we leave. That was the first time I ever saw an American dollar.

All this time we had to keep the news hidden from everywhere but the closest family and friends. People would inevitably get jealous and start asking questions and causing trouble. It's the nature of people, especially where resources are so limited. Why should this family get to go to the United States and not me? So we knew to keep everything quiet. All the kids understood that message. They followed my lead and said nothing. Even Mohammed in private school with his wealthy friends said nothing. And certainly no one in the neighborhood knew. The other the reason we said nothing: We were never quite sure if the whole thing was true, if we were actually going. We'd been let down so many times before.

Yet neighbors couldn't help seeing our new shopping bags. They noticed when I tried to sell some of our old clothes and housewares. It wasn't yet the holiday of Eid, when everyone buys gifts and new clothes after Ramadan. So the children's friends started asking why. Why the new clothes now? Why, when you never did before? What's going on? We had to make up a story. I told the neighbors, and told all the kids to tell the neighbors if they asked, that we were preparing to go to Jordan to see a doctor for Abdulaziz. It was what you call a "white lie." People would come and visit and say, Good luck in Jordan, I hope you find help there. Some gave me the names of relatives or friends who lived in Amman. I took the names and thanked them. What could I do? Then one day an Iraqi man from the IOM showed up at our apartment unannounced. He'd been sent to investigate us and make sure our story was true, that everyone was who we said they were. Because sometimes people will invent family relationships in order to get visas or papers. They were just being cautious, but it alarmed us. He'd been snooping around the neighborhood asking everyone questions about us. Where did we live, what did we do, how many kids where there, where was their father? All these questions. Since there were no real street addresses in that part of Sana'a, he apparently got lost, and had to call me minutes before he arrived. He needed directions to our house!

He pretended he was coming to help us. But we knew better the moment he showed up. He asked us a lot of questions. If these were really my children. *How could they not be,* I wondered. The embassy had already taken our DNA!

After the guy left, he apparently went around the neighborhood again asking questions. There was a small, popular place around the corner that sold rotisserie chickens and we were friends with the owner. He walked into the place and asked the owner about us in front of a bunch of customers. I don't know, maybe the owner was having a bad day. But he told the Iraqi guy to get lost. *Why you asking me about neighbors? No one knows you here. You're not even Yemeni.* He kicked the guy out of his shop. We heard the whole story later.

Once we checked out with the investigator, we were told nothing was holding us up anymore. They said we'd leave in seven days. It was the month of Ramadan by then, and we'd been trying to fast during the days. Ramadan normally makes the days go slow, but it was July that month and hot, and each hour felt like torture. Every day felt like a month. We waited and prepared. We fasted and prayed. The night finally came before we were supposed to go. We hardly slept. In the morning we were so excited and all packed. But then the phone rang. It was the IOM. Our flight was canceled, they said. A bird had flown into the engine of the plane so the plane wasn't going anywhere. They would let us know when a new flight was scheduled. They said nothing else and hung up.

The kids looked at me. I didn't even know what to say. I tried to explain. The bird. The engine. The flight. It sounded like they were just making up a story. We all tried to figure it out. "Maybe they're just scamming us?" Mohammed said. But why would they give us the money for clothes, we wondered. Why take fingerprints? In the end we didn't really know anything about these people. We had no experience at all with international organizations. We spent all day puzzling over the bird, the engine, the sudden cancellation. Maybe we weren't going anywhere.

We didn't sleep that night. The next morning, they called and said there'd be another flight in a week. We had to wait again. Yet at some point that day or the day after we learned about the bird in the engine. It was true. It had been reported in the newspapers. A bird actually did disable an airplane. Of course, it had to be our plane!

It's hard for me even now to talk about the next seven days. The worry, the waiting. The not knowing. The neighbors. You have to remember that the war was going on then in Yemen. There was fighting all over. The president had fled the country. The group from the north was trying to come over to the south. We didn't want to get stuck again in a civil war. And each day it was more and more dangerous. Those seven days were the longest days in my life. Anything could change. The airport could close, the city shut down. I'm sure, in the back of my mind, were memories of Mogadishu, the trauma I'd already been through with my parents.

The day finally came. The phone rang. We were to meet at the American embassy that evening. From there a bus would take us to the airport. We'd be flying that night out of Yemen.

With the exception of my parents, most people still thought we were only flying to Jordan to see a doctor for Abdulaziz. But now it was time to tell them the truth. I called our friends and family, the ones I trusted most. I told them about going to the United States, that they had to keep it secret until we left. I was afraid someone or something still might ruin our plans. But I rented a van for family and friends so they could come with us and have a proper goodbye at the airport.

We packed and fasted all day. I cooked and friends cooked to make a meal for *Iftar*, the breaking of the fast. We all piled in a van and met at

the American Embassy. It was evening by then. The sun was going down.
Because it was *Iftar*, the streets were empty, everyone inside their houses
breaking the fast. We got off at the embassy and put our bags by the front
security gate, and the people told us to wait for the bus that would take
us to the airport. We broke the fast for the last time with our family and
friends and neighbors right outside, on the street in front of the American
embassy. It was a joyous occasion.

Soon the bus appeared. We loaded our bags. Friends and neighbors
were crying. We held on to each other. There were three or four other
families we were traveling with, about 30 of us altogether. They gave us
IOM identification cards to wear around our necks. We waved through
the bus windows and then we were moving. Everyone slid away. It was
getting dark now. I was still thinking the whole thing could be a joke. I
was still waiting for something to go wrong.

We flew first from Sana'a to Rome. It was the first time any of us had
been on a plane. The kids were looking all around in disbelief. We stayed
inside the aircraft in Italy while it was being cleaned. They didn't want
the refugee families to leave the plane. From Rome we flew to Frankfurt.
We had to wait for a wheelchair for Abdulaziz so our family was the last
off the plane. He needed diapers, too, so we took our time inside the
plane. We had six hours to transit out of Germany. By the time we got into
the terminal it was late at night and no one was around. The place was
empty. The few people there didn't speak Arabic or English. Certainly
not Somali. And all the other refugee families we'd been traveling with,
who we were supposed to stay together with, had gone. We were alone.
We didn't know where to go.

We tried to find someone to help us. It was late, and no one seemed to
care. They just looked at us as if we shouldn't be there. No one was particularly friendly. Most people just ignored us.

We walked one way, then another. We couldn't find our group. The
whole time we got more and more lost. I started freaking out. I was sure
we were going to be left behind. Then some guy, an American, recognized
the label on our bags, the IOM symbol, and said he'd help us find our
group. He took us to another section of the airport. Mohammed saw a
Somali kid running and he took off after him. Then we all did, the whole

family in the Frankfurt airport, running after this one Somali boy as if our life depended on it! Which, in some ways, it did.

When we were reunited with the others, we learned that the IOM people were looking for us. They made everyone stay in one place while they searched the airport. We were exhausted by then. The IOM people brought us to a place where we were able to lie down and rest. We weren't leaving for another five hours.

We weren't flying directly to the United States. Because of the war in Yemen, the Americans couldn't travel to Sana'a for our final interviews. So, they told us back in Yemen, we'd have to fly to Romania first and stay there in a transit center for a few months while our applications were finalized. We didn't think much of it at the time, but now that we were in the airport in Frankfurt, we learned we were flying to a place called Timisoara. But to get to this Timisoara we had to fly first to Bucharest, which we did later that day. Yet, once we arrived in Bucharest, there wasn't enough room on the plane for all the Somali families. They had to leave some of us behind. Of course, it was our family who they left behind. We were always the last ones!

We waited all day for the night flight. I wanted to call my mother back in Sana'a to let her know we were okay, but we had no phone. I asked Mohammed to ask the guy who was helping us if we could borrow his phone. Mohammed was shy and didn't want to do it, so I had to go up to him and make the gesture with my palm and point to his phone. He was kind enough to let me use it. He actually helped me make the call. I told my mom we were okay, Mashallah, there are good people in the world.

It was nighttime when we arrived in Timisoara. We got on a bus and drove through the dark. We thought we were going to a hotel or a house, but we arrived at a place that looked like prison. It had fences all around and a caged door and security guards. We all looked at each other and said nothing. All of us were afraid. Where is this place they're taking us? It looked like we were going to a work camp or maybe a jail.

They let us off the bus. It was very cold. There were a bunch of people milling around inside the building. Africans and Asians, Syrians and Iraqis. We were brought to one room with concrete floors and metal bunk beds, all of us put in the same room. The kids were scared because the place was old and run-down. I could see their disappointment. They expected more. This was not America. But I was relieved to be there. So what if the place was cold and ugly? We got out of Yemen safely, away from the war. We were in a new place. On the table in the room, the people had left us food and drink, juices and bread, and diapers for Abdulaziz. Everything we needed was there, and lots of it—things I'd struggled my whole life to have.

They brought us cooked food that night but I was afraid to eat it. I didn't know if they knew we were Muslim, and they might have put pork in the food. So we just stared at the food and each other and didn't eat it, even though we were all hungry. We were all exhausted anyhow. I fell fast asleep.

The next morning when we woke up, we heard kids outside in the hallway. Mohammed and Abdullah left the room to explore. There were all these children running around, a lot of Somali families—some of the people who'd been with us in the airport in Germany. They'd arrived a day or two before. And there were lots of others just like us, refugees from around the world. Each family had their own room with bunk beds and, though it looked like jail, it was actually fine. There was a shared kitchen for all the women, a playground for the kids, a room with a computer. Though Romania is one of the poorest countries in Europe, it looked rich and beautiful to us. There were green trees outside. The sky was blue that first day. Everything was clean. We were happy to be there and grateful to have come that far.

The IOM facility was gated and and tightly controlled. We could go in and out but always through a security check. We had a schedule. For the next few weeks, they brought us food and water each morning. The staff then broke us into two or three groups and would take us into the city to go shopping or see the downtown. We didn't know how long we'd be at the IOM facility. They told us initially six months maximum, but we quickly learned people had been stuck at that facility for three years. Some five years. I didn't mind. We were safe and I was busy during the day and the children were taken care of. In the morning we had appointments; sometimes they brought us to the hospital or to see doctors. Or we went to teach people how to cook our food. In Timisoara they taught us how to drive a car. I drove my first car in Romania! They showed us how to make clothing at a factory. Each day at two in the afternoon they brought us back to the facility and all of us moms went to the kitchen and started cooking. In those days, after I put dinner on the table for the kids, I would lie down on the bunkbed and think about all those years in Yemen and Somalia. It felt so good to be in a place where I didn't worry every second of the day. I thanked God for helping us through the hard times. It was the first time in my entire life I was able to just lie down in the afternoon.

Those first few months in Romania it was still the summer. The days were very hot and there were mosquitos. But when summer ended and the fall began, it started getting cold. That was our first real experience with cold. It was nothing like the cold in Yemen. It was truly freezing. Our jackets only helped so much.

In the facility all the families took classes. They taught us things about the United States. What to expect, what to do. How to get help. We had a swearing in, too, where we had to take an oath and tell the truth. At one end of the building there was a pin-up board where they put the notices. They were putting up notices every few weeks for the families who'd been approved to travel. Their names and their destinations and the dates of travel. Whenever these posts went up, everyone ran to the board to see if their name was on the list. Our name was never on the list.

As the months went by and winter came, the kids started asking: When are we going to America? Are we *ever* really going to America? Mohammed especially was growing impatient. In Yemen he'd had a very good chance of becoming a soccer star. They were already paying him to play in a semi-professional league. He sacrificed what he had there to stay with the family and come to the United States. At first, when he learned there was a chance through the IOM that we'd get out of Yemen, he was excited. He thought, *Great, we'll be sent somewhere in Europe where I can try to play professional soccer.* He was that good. But then he learned we were going to America. No one played soccer in America. So he felt a little let down. And now we were stuck in Romania. He felt as if he were in jail. He lost patience. They all did. I told them: As long as I don't have to worry about making money and getting food and medicine to the kids, as long as I get to rest in the afternoon, we are fine. But that wasn't enough for the kids.

For weeks, then months, every time they posted names on the board, we ran over to see. Each time we were disappointed. Others we knew were leaving or had already left. Beside their names were dates and cities: New

York. Chicago. Boston. San Diego. Each time the family would celebrate, and we'd walk back to our room and hope for the next time. It kept going like that for a long time. Almost all the people we'd initially flown over with from Yemen were gone. Just a few families remained. We were one of them. Then one day it was there, listed: *Fardusa Abdullah Abdo*. Our destination: *Vermont*.

We were confused. We had never heard the name "Vermont." Mohammed and Abdullah ran to the computer. They went on the internet and put in the name. The first thing that came up on the screen for Vermont was a photograph of cows. Then more cows! There were no photographs of beautiful cities or luxurious streets. No oceans or plazas or glass skyscrapers. Just old houses and cows. The kids kept looking at the internet. They were like, Damn, what is this place, Vermont? Why do we always have to be different from other people? Why are we going to a place fit for cows? But on the computer, Mohammed told me later, he saw a photograph of Vermont in fall, all the colors on the trees, and the mountains, and that made his heart lift a little. It looked peaceful at least, he said, peaceful and beautiful. Maybe it wouldn't be so bad after all.

Normally when a family was leaving the facility in Romania, they'd have plenty of time to get ready and pack and relax. But in our case, new Somali families were arriving and they needed our room right away. We had to pack quickly and clean the room and get everyone ready. We had only a matter of hours. Then we had to wait outside in the playground with all our bags. Then we saw an enormous group of Somalis walking in, a new group. They looked as confused as we were when we first arrived months earlier and saw the cages and fences. We said goodbye to our friends there, the people we'd been living with for five months. It was the last time we'd see them.

Back In Yemen people told us: When you go to the US, they will put you in a big house and you will have a car, maybe two cars, parked beside the house, and when you go to the kitchen, they will have three types of sinks. One for water, one for orange juice, and another for milk. We'd be in a kind of paradise, and you don't need to worry about anything.

So we had big expectations when we arrived in the United States. But arriving in Vermont was nothing we could have expected. It was winter and bitterly cold and there was no city below when we landed. Abdirashid Hussein met us at the small airport. We had to split up in two cars, we were so many. We drove away from the airport. There was nothing out there in the night, just darkness and woods, a few lights. We drove into downtown Burlington. Our apartment was on the third floor of a house. It was difficult getting Abdulaziz up there. We wouldn't be able to stay in that apartment long. The house itself felt fragile, as if it might fall apart when we walked on the wood boards. Mohammed and Abdullah went to the kitchen. They checked out the sink. They were disappointed when they didn't find the three taps, the one for orange juice, the one for milk, the other for water.

Sometime later that night, after Abdirashid left and we were getting settled, I looked out the window. It was snowing. I'd never seen snow before. I shouted to the kids, and we crowded around the window and watched this thing. We'd only seen snow in the movies. We watched it for a long time out the window. Some of the kids went outside and tried to make snowballs. I stayed inside with Abdulaziz. When they came back, their hands were frozen and Zainab was crying. She later got sick. It wasn't at all what they expected of snow. They didn't know how much it would hurt their hands.

But then our life started changing again. We found another house, in Winooski, closer to town, where we could walk to places. It was big enough and had access for Abdulaziz. We met new people, and the workers at the resettlement office became a part of our life. And whatever story was there before, we left it behind, and we began a new chapter and turned a new page.

Abdihamid

My family herded camels in Somalia. There were many names for people like us: *reer miyi* or *reer badia,* people of the countryside or scrubland. *Reer guuraaga,* nomads or the people who roved around. But the name I like best is *qoraax joog* which means something like "people who stay outdoors in beauty." *Qoraax* means sunlight in Somali and also can mean "beautiful." So the life we lived outdoors staying with animals was a beautiful life, especially because of our camels.

To understand my background you have to understand the importance of the camel in Somali culture. People who own camels are held in high esteem in Somalia. They have a different life than others and a different connection to the world. They are independent and self-reliant and walk everywhere with their camels to see the world. They make their own food, use their camels for milk and meat, and feed others they come in contact with. For this reason, there are many songs and folktales, poems and stories about camels and camel herders in Somalia. When you take care of a camel you pull the camel behind you in a respectful way and the camel learns to follow you. You don't lead them from behind or hit them like you do with a cow, so it is a relationship of respect and trust, this big creature following you around as a partner. A camel can walk for weeks without water. Like us, they are great travelers. Their milk is the healthiest food in the world.

My family was well off. We owned 100 camels. We had goats, sheep, and cows, too. While the women and the young people stayed in one place with the sheep and goats not far from the capital, my father and brothers and me—when I was old enough—traveled with the camels. We walked one way in the dry season and another during the rains. We moved each year between three countries—Somalia, Ethiopia, and Kenya. In this way we made a big circle over the course of the year. Somalia to Ethiopia, then back through Kenya to Somalia again. Six months going one way, six months the other. Because our families had been herding camels there for centuries, we had rights of movement from the King of Ethiopia. We knew no borders. We would go all the way from Mogadishu to Dolo and Godey in Ethiopia and down to Moyale on the border of Kenya. If there were no rains, we stayed up north and west in Ethiopia. The people knew us there and welcomed us. The border people always let us pass. One side or the other, it was all the same country once, and Somali people lived on both sides before England and Italy split the countries.

We loved our camels. Each one had his or her own name and personality. They wore wooden bells. The head camel, the *naag*, is a female, the herd queen. She wore the biggest bell, which the others could hear and follow. *Koor* was the name of the big bell. We had different calls and whistles for different things to communicate with the camels. A low *oooohh*. A high *whoop whoop whoop*. They always understood what we were saying. *Come back to camp. Let's go home.* Or, *Water ahead.* We spoke the same language. They also understood some of our songs. We had milking songs. Watering songs. Songs to bring them in at night. I can remember the songs to this day, especially the watering song. It was always a beautiful moment when we sang the watering song and the camels came close and we pulled up water from the well and the camels drank for the first time in weeks or months. They knew the song and would get excited and we would, too. We would stay by the well for 24 hours, drinking and rejoicing, and then they'd be full and happy and ready to move on.

During birthing season we always had to be in a safe place because it takes a week for a camel baby to walk on its own. Once, while traveling, we were in a dangerous place when a young mother went into labor. It was her first time giving birth and she didn't know exactly what to do and she just stopped in the middle of the road. We tried to get her to move on, but she wouldn't move and had her baby right there in the road. We were traveling between camps, in a place where there were lions. it was late afternoon and starting to get dark. Normally we would have made camp, but we couldn't stay in that area. We had to take her baby and carry him to a safer place. It took three of us to carry the baby camel and the mother screamed and kicked the whole time. A more experienced mother would've known to trust us but she was too young. It took us a whole day to carry the baby to a safe place and then we were able to make camp and rest and let the mother nurse her baby and wait the seven days so we could move on.

We traveled very lightly with only the essentials: a wood bucket, a *haan*, for milking. An axe for firewood and making fences out of trees. A flashlight to see at night and to scare off hyenas and lions. Jerry cans for water. A sheet of plastic for shelter. We all carried knives. We also had one rifle between us. Every family did. Ours was a Hawken rifle, the old powder type, which could only shoot one bullet at a time. But it was enough to protect us because lions could smell the scent of the gun and that was enough to keep them away.

When we moved to a new place, one of the adults would go ahead and walk for two days or so to see what was around and if there was food or water ahead for the camels. We called this man the *sahan*, the scout. If he found a good place for our camp, he'd walk back and then we'd all go there and stay for a while. We'd make little huts to sleep in and a thorn enclosure for the animals, a *haero*, to keep them penned and safe for the night. Sometimes just the older and younger animals stayed inside the *haero* while the adults stayed outside.

Often we camped near small towns or villages. We knew the people there and they knew us. We'd stay there for a few days or sometimes a few weeks. We traded with the people for food or batteries, sugar or tea or whatever we needed; and we in turn would give them milk. Sometimes at night we'd get together with them in a circle and share stories and songs and poems. Different occasions meant different stories or songs. A ceremony or a wedding or the time of the year. The elders would tell how certain things happened or how a place got its name, how to tell a wet season was coming or a dry year. Every culture has its way of teaching and learning and that was our way, passing on knowledge in a circle around a fire. The songs were called *hees*, the poems *gabay*. Children loved the rhyming songs; there were so many. And they learned through folktales, too. Stories and riddles we called *sheeko* or *sheekoharir*.

One night sitting around with others we saw the lights of an airplane high in the sky. *What were those people up there looking for,* I wondered. "They must be hungry," I said. Going all over the place searching for food. Just like us. Why else would they be up there, traveling that way? Little did I know back then that one day I'd be one of those people up in a plane, too.

One day when I was very young, back with my mother and the other children, a lion leaped on one of our cows. I was only a few feet away. I'd never seen a lion before. I didn't even know what one looked like. For that reason I wasn't scared. I just stood close, watching. The lion held the back of the cow. The cow was trying to escape. I remember the crunching sound. The bite of the lion on the leg bone. Then the lion looked at me, this little kid. Why wasn't I afraid? Maybe I was crazy? He didn't like me being so close. So he backed off, long enough for the cow to escape. At that point my family came running and shouting and the lion ran away. My parents were amazed that the lion hadn't attacked me, that I was still standing right there, unafraid. I really had no idea what I was looking at, but everyone seemed happy. I wasn't eaten! The cow wasn't eaten! There's a saying in Somalia: The only one who can defeat the lion is he who does not know the lion. I can tell you from personal experience the saying is true. I didn't know the lion back then—but now I do.

The first 17 years of my life passed that way, living outdoors with the camels, in the *qoraax joog*. I was healthy and strong. Our daily life was all about finding food for the animals and ourselves. If you didn't move, you didn't survive. I knew little about the rest of the world or the news. I knew the animals and the weather, the Koran, the stars. We didn't concern ourselves with who was the president and the government or what was happening in the capital. We didn't follow any of that.

There's so much I don't remember about when the war began, so much I don't wish to recall of that time when our lives changed forever. Strangers came and pointed guns at us and said, "Kill the animal and cook it for us." What could we do? We had only the one old rifle between us. These men, they had guns. They outnumbered us. We didn't even know who they wore. Soldiers, bandits. Opportunists. People who knew we had many animals and could just take them. Which they did. They took our cows, our sheep, our goats. They took our camels. They tried to take us but we escaped.

We ran first to the capital where we thought we'd be safe and find help. But no one was in charge in the city. There was no government. No police—the war had come there, too. We stayed at our family's homes. There were ten of us: my father and brothers and their wives and children. Gunmen came there. They shot my father. They shot my brother Ismail. They were both killed right in front of us. We ran out of the house. We had to get out of the city. We had to go south. It's hard to think about even now, what happened that day and the next few days. Trying to get out of the city, trying to go to Kismayo. At one point my cousin was shot in the leg, and his brother refused to leave him. They both were killed. At another point we were in a car. There were checkpoints. We were pulled over and told to sit on the ground. A guy pointed a gun at us and was about to shoot us all, but another guy, the leader of the group, showed up in a truck and yelled at the guy with the gun. They had an argument. The leader told us to go. We all got up and ran into the car, but the driver was so scared, he couldn't get the car to start. That was a horrible feeling. We were all so terrified. We just got out and walked and left the car behind.

We were the fortunate ones. They didn't kill us that day. We joined with others walking south. There were maybe 20 of us who stuck together. At one point we saw the government cars passing us on the road, the bigwigs, the army commander, fleeing south, too. We knew then there was nothing safe in the capital anymore.

We ended up walking for weeks. Mogadishu to Agoye, Agoye to Shalan Boot. Shalan Boot to Kismayo. Sometimes we got a lift in a truck, but mostly we went by foot. It was safer to keep off the roads. We had no food. Sometimes no water. People got sick along the way. Sometimes people would find something to eat, a goat maybe, and share a meal. But a lot of people died on the way. There were militiamen and bandits who killed for no reason. Anyone who feared God had already left the country. It was safer to travel in the forest with the lions. Between the men and the lions, we chose the lions.

It took us a month to make it to Kenya. The Kenyan people welcomed us. We were taken to a refugee camp on the coast. In Marafa Camp I lived with my brother and his family. We lived in tents. We even had electricity. We lived there for five years until they closed the camp and sent us to western Kenya. Kakuma was a huge camp in the middle of nowhere filled with refugees from all over Africa. There was nothing in Kakuma but a big highway that connected Sudan to Kenya. We lived inside a fence, like a zoo. And since there was no work there, and nothing to do, I spent most of my time hanging out by the highway, just watching through the fence the trucks passing, and waving at the truck drivers. That became my life, so different from before. It was like jail.

In Kakuma we lived in areas by nationality. Somali people in one place, Sudanese in another. Burundi people. Rwandans. Eritreans or Ugandans. I became friends with people from all over, particularly Sudan. Outside the camp lived the Turkana people. Some of them worked inside the camp. We often traded with them, rations of our rice or spaghetti for firewood or other things they could get outside of the camp. It was hard to communicate because we spoke different languages. Our cultures, too, were very different. Once we traded some chili spice—some *pili pili*—with a Turkana man. He'd never tried our kind of spice before, and when he tasted it, he choked and thought we were trying to poison him! He even went to the police and said, "Look, they're trying to kill me!" When he showed the policeman the "poison," the policeman saw it was just dried chili pepper. We all had a good laugh—but not the Turkana man.

Do you know what it's like for someone who used to walk their camels all over the country, free of borders, to be fenced in a refugee camp? Suddenly you're locked inside a dusty place, given rations. There's nothing to do. No animals to keep you company and care for. You can't make your own food. You become reliant on others.

Maybe that's why, while living in Kakuma, I first became ill. I would get dizzy sometimes and feel lightheaded. It happened when I looked at the horizon or when I was up in a high place. I didn't know what it was: the dizziness, the pain in my stomach. The feeling that my body was just dropping. I couldn't eat. The doctor at the camp gave me medicine. They said it was because of all I'd been through. This illness made it hard to do anything physical. Not that there was any work in the camp to begin with.

In Kakuma, me and my brother and family all applied for asylum to whatever country would take us. We waited there seven years. In 2008 my brother and his wife left with some of their children. They were accepted to go to America. I was left behind with one of their children, my nephew. Sometime later my nephew was sent to America, and I was the only one of the family left behind. I thought at first they didn't want the whole family to go together in one plane for our own safety, in case the plane crashed. That's why they split us up in three. It turned out that wasn't the case at all. It was just part of the waiting, part of the paperwork, and mine took a lot longer.

I waited another four months, five months. After seven months I began to worry. Maybe they weren't letting me go. Maybe I'd be stuck in Kakuma forever. I went with a friend to the doctor. My friend, too, had been waiting for his name to be posted. I asked the doctor if there was something wrong. He took my ID number and checked. He said there was nothing wrong, my papers were in order. I shouldn't worry. I'd find out in a few days. We left the doctor's office and later that afternoon my name was posted. It was really happening. I was leaving. But my friend's name was not posted. So while I was happy, I felt bad for him. I would be leaving, but he would not.

I had no idea what the other side of the world looked like. We had some training before we left. Five months, where they showed us movies and told us things about America and what good families do and what bad ones do. They introduced us to buildings and houses and told us about school and having to pay for housing. I wasn't scared because of what I'd already been through. Maybe a bit nervous because I had a lot to learn, but mostly I was happy. Happy to start a new life in a new place but a little sad for the people I was leaving behind in the camp, the friends I'd made there.

I left Kakuma in the middle of June. We flew to London first. Then I got on another plane to New York. I was with a bunch of other Somali people, but when we got to New York City, they were all going to other places. Ohio or Minnesota or Texas. I was the only one going to Vermont. I was suddenly left alone in the airport. The guy who was helping us gave me my ticket and told me what gate to go to. But I was afraid. I couldn't remember the name "Vermont." I couldn't even say it out loud. And the airport was so big and so many people were rushing one way or another. I felt lost, unable to even pronounce the name of my destination. So the guy took me to the gate and hung my ticket around my neck and said, "Don't worry. Stay here. You're in the right place."

The flight to Burlington didn't take long. Everyone got off the plane and I was the last one on, just sitting there, waiting. The pilot was standing by the door. I asked him if knew where the IOM person was. He said to walk through the gate and someone will be there on the other side. I was tired and freezing. It was late at night. June 15. Even though it was springtime in Vermont, it felt incredibly cold. Then I forgot about my bag. I didn't know how to get it. A nice guy saw I was in trouble, and he took my ticket and showed me where to go, to the baggage claim, and I found my bag there going in a circle. I wish I knew who that guy was today. I never got to thank him.

I waited some more, alone with my bag. I was worried no one was coming. I saw a Black guy staring at me. But he didn't look like someone who spoke Somali. The man came over and introduced himself in Somali. He was Abdirashid Hussein, my case worker. Boy was I happy! We've been good friends ever since.

He drove me that night to my family in Winooski. It was after midnight. Everyone woke up and we had a big reunion and ate food and no one slept all night. That was the beginning of my new life in Vermont.

When I first arrived, I tried working. I found a job at a factory in Winooski where they made soap and body wash. I worked on the line. It was a ten-hour shift, at Twincraft Skincare. You had to be quick and watching the machine all the time, the line with the little bottles and the shampoo, and everything moving so fast, it made me dizzy. Being inside that building, the smell, the light, the watching the line moving all the time—I couldn't do it. I would get dizzy. I felt I was falling all the time. The same sickness I had in Kakuma came back or never went away. I felt bad about getting sick, but I had to stop working. I physically wasn't able.

Still, I really loved Burlington right away. Not the cold, but the people. Everyone was so kind. Everyone helped us. The resettlement people, the assistance. I was so grateful then, especially when I couldn't work. I will never forget how people helped, how they saved my family. How they saved me. How they brought me here.

One day that first summer I was walking in Burlington. I didn't know about the summer holiday, Independence Day. I was out on the streets when I heard a loud explosion. I nearly dropped to the ground. I thought the war had started again. I got really scared, but people were smiling in the streets. I didn't understand. It was evening. The sound kept coming. The crack of gunfire and bombs. I ran home frightened and locked the door and hid. It was only afterwards I learned about July Fourth and fireworks! It still freaks me out a little, even though I know it's an important American holiday. I still don't like to hear the sound.

I've been here now over ten years. I get up at three in the morning for *Fajr*, morning prayers. Then I listen to the news on the radio or TV. I go to mosque each day. Sometimes many times a day if I can make the prayer times. I go to the small mosque in Winooski where most of the Somali people go, but also to the larger mosque in South Burlington where a lot of Arab people or Afghani or Bosnians go. I like going to one then the other. I see friends there. I learned to drive a few years ago, but I still like walking. I walk all over the place. At least I do in the warm months. You can see so much more of life when you walk. When you drive, you just pass everything by; walking is better. I guess it's how I used to travel when I was young.

Each day I usually go to Nimo's store, the halal store on North Street. Sometimes I shop at Costco or eat lunch at Kismayo Kitchen. My family, my brother and wife and their children, left Vermont in 2015. They moved to Minnesota, but I wanted to stay here. It was a little sad at the time, but we've been through so much over the years, and I've moved around so much in my life, that I wanted to stay in one place. I was happy here in Burlington. People move on. Life goes on. That period of time, I didn't get really sad because here, in the United States, everyone can do whatever they like. If they want to move, that's fine. If you want to stay here, that's okay, too. We are still connected. I talk with my family on the phone all the time; I see all their faces on WhatsApp. I talk to friends back in Kenya, people I knew in the camp. And here I have my community. I teach Koran a few times a week to kids. I try to tell them about Somalia, a place they've never been, and about the life we had. It gives me hope, teaching the young people.

I still dream of camels. Walking with them. Milking them. Sometimes I'll watch videos on YouTube about camels and Somalia and watch the old clips of the songs we used to sing while bringing up water from the wells for our herds. I grew up with those songs. *Hees geela marka la waraabinayo.* Words that mean basically: *You are strong and we pray to God to keep you strong and find places that have lots of food. We seek the same for both us, give birth and have a healthy baby.* It makes me smile to hear the old songs, to see the camels. The freedom they have, the freedom I had back then.

A lot of people come to Burlington and leave because it is too small or too cold or they can't find housing or a job. But I love it here. I love Vermont. I love America. I can't imagine going any place else. I came to America a sick man. I suffered from that illness a long time but now I'm better. Sometimes I'll remember the shooting and the killings back home but then I'll wake up and think: *That is over now. That part of my life is finished. I am here, a new part has begun.* I am so grateful for being here. My age doesn't matter. I am optimistic about the future. About working again, about teaching young people about their culture and language. I think all the time about how I can make my future better and help my family and friends. Honestly, I love America and the generous people. I can understand 50 percent of what people say in English. I am still learning.

I've traveled back to Kenya a few times since I came here. I visit old friends and see how they are doing and in Nairobi I go to the Somali neighborhood, which feels a lot like home. I've traveled to Saudi Arabia, too. But I'm still afraid of going back to Somalia itself. I've gone very close to the border, in Kenya, but will not cross over. I feel it is still too dangerous, still too unsafe. Anything can happen there.

I'm also proud of the way we used to live before everything fell apart. Our nomadic lifestyle. Our *qoraax joog*, staying outdoors, under the sun, living a beautiful lifestyle, for it was beautiful, the land and the animals and the food we made for ourselves. We gave our milk away to people whose land we passed through. It was better to give it away, to prevent anyone being jealous of you and giving you the evil eye. So we were good to others and people were good to us and the camels were good for the land. Everyone benefited. We knew all the other animals too—the hyenas and lions and the elephants—and they knew us.

I still try to keep track of those animals in the news. I'm especially interested in the elephants. I look them up on the computer to see how they are doing. Before the war, thousands of elephants lived in Somalia. But when the war came most of them fled south across the border to Kenya—just like us. They knew it was too dangerous to stay on their own grounds and migrated to Kenya. Somali elephants are different than the Kenyan elephants in how they look and act. But most were able to survive in Kenya in ways they couldn't across the border. If you go to Kenya today, you can see the Somali elephants. Scientists have been tracking them with radios over the years. They are very smart animals. They want to return to their homeland but can still sense the danger across the border. They can hear things hundreds of miles away. They can smell the war. The guns, the ammunition. They know when and where men are armed and where it isn't safe to go. They can feel the bad things, the places where their parents or brothers or sisters were killed.

Yes, thousands of elephants once lived in Somalia but none has been there in over 20 years. Recently I heard this: A few years ago one of the Somali elephants the scientists were tracking in Kenya left his grazing grounds along the Kenyan coast and headed north to Somalia. The elephant was an older male, around 30 years old. He walked 137 miles in 18 days. He traveled at night and hid in the forest during the day from poachers. He made it all the way to Somalia. No one expected it. No one had ever seen that before. Because of his age, the scientists thought he'd recalled the old route back home, the old migration path that had been disrupted by war. He was the first recorded elephant to return to Somalia in 20 years. But he didn't stay. He must have known the country was still not safe.

In less than 24 hours, he headed back to Kenya.

Afterword

*D*eep North began as a storytelling project in 2019 organized by Somali community leader Abdirashid Hussein, community organizer Laurie Stavrand, and myself, a writer and novelist. Our intention was to preserve for the next generations the histories of people forced to flee their homeland who'd subsequently resettled in Vermont. I met Abdirashid and Laurie while researching a novel about a Somali asylum seeker. Both Laurie and Abdirashid worked then at the US Committee for Refugees and Immigrants in Colchester, Vermont. Abdirashid's passion, insight and hard work on behalf of new Americans coupled with Laurie's outreach and my own interest in storytelling led directly to the project and this book.

The three stories published here are the result of multiple recording sessions both in-person and over Zoom over a period of five years between 2019 and 2023. Shadir Mohamed spoke directly for himself in English while a translator was employed for Fardusa Abdo and Abdihamid Muhamud. Our translator, not by accident, was Fardusa's oldest son, Mohammed Abdo, a 27-year-old man who, up until the time of the recording sessions, had never heard his mother's story. Listening to his mother's story and having to tell it back in his own words was a revelation for Mohammed. She'd never previously talked about her past or the war or what she'd been through, and we were fully aware that recounting traumatic memories can often retraumatize; yet telling her story in a structured setting, in the comfort of her home, among family and supportive witnesses (Laurie and I were always in the "room") turned out to be a real gift, not only for Fardusa but also for Mohammed and the witnesses. During the sessions we all felt the palpable pain and release, the occasional recounting of joy, and the relief of the story told, witnessed, and recorded for future generations.

Abdihamid, likewise, rarely spoke of his past, and Shadir too had never shared his story with his children. Why had their stories never been narrated before? Once their lives changed forever in the spring of 1991, Shadir, Fardusa, and Abdihamid never had time to look back. Each day was an act of survival. Even when they reached the relative safety of Winooski or Burlington, there were bills to pay, children to feed, a language to learn, a bewildering bureaucracy, and new culture to navigate. Retrospection was a luxury they never had. They came to Vermont with a label, and of all the labels for someone who's lost their home *refugee* might be the most damning; it means they've lost not only their home and their country but the entire cultural context that once gave them meaning as a person. How does one lose the label and become seen again as individual? One way is through stories. Stories and memories: the two things they were able to carry with them when everything else was stripped from them.

In Abdirashid Hussein's words: "The intention of telling these stories and the intention of this book is to reach and educate the American public about who refugees are. When people learn their stories, what their life was like before, who they were and what they did, they will see them not just as the label but as real people who had backgrounds and professions before they ended up refugees. Three people from Somalia are telling their stories here but the subject of this book goes beyond them and their stories. This book is for the millions of people stuck right now in refugee camps, to show how rich and varied and vital their lives were before they were forced from their homes. We want to show how, when resettlement is done right, refugees can regain both their lives and their dignity."

This book couldn't have been accomplished without the help of Mohammed Abdo, who served as translator and also conceived of and drew the cover art for the book. Mohammed's own story is worthy of another chapter (if not another book). He lives now in Colchester as a designer and artist and works with children with disabilities. The printing of this book was made possible by a grant from the Vermont Humanities Council.

Brad Kessler
Sandgate, Vermont, 2023

Shadir in 1996 at Swaleh Nguru in Utanga Refugee Camp in Kenya

Printed in the USA
CPSIA information can be obtained
at www.ICGtesting.com
LVHW092338281223
767703LV00038B/562